The Elder Black

E. Percil Stanford

With the Assistance of

Mrs. Ida Mae Hoggard
Mrs. Monja Thorton
Mr. Anthony Morrell
Mrs. Bernice Rollins
Community Interviewers

and

Mr. John Jones
Community Consultant

Center on Aging, San Diego State University

The Elder Black

A CROSS-CULTURAL STUDY OF MINORITY ELDERS IN SAN DIEGO

Editor & Project Director:	Ramón Valle, PhD
Project Director:	James Ajemian, PhD (First Year)
Associate Editor:	Charles Martinez, MSW
Secretaries:	Mrs. Peggy King Mrs. Patricia Murphy Mrs. Alicia Nevarez-Krotky Ms. Cynthia Wright
Cover:	Mr. Calvin Woo, Humangraphics
Published By:	Center on Aging School of Social Work San Diego State University
Design Style & Phototypeset:	Betty R. Truitt Word Processing Center San Diego State University

Monographs and Technical Reports Series

The Elder American Indian:	Frank Dukepoo, PhD
The Elder Black:	E. Percil Stanford, PhD
The Elder Chinese:	Ms. Eva Cheng, MSSW
The Elder Guamanian:	Wesley H. Ishikawa, DSW
The Elder Japanese:	Ms. Karen C. Ishizuka, MSW
The Elder Latino:	Ramón Valle, PhD Ms. Lydia Mendoza, MS
The Elder Pilipino:	Ms. Roberta Peterson, MSSW
The Elder Samoan:	Wesley H. Ishikawa, DSW

Project Supported by Funds from U.S. Department of Health, Education and Welfare, Office of Human Development, Administration on Aging. Grant Number AoA-90-A-317, Mr. David Dowd, Project Officer AoA, OHD, DHEW.

Distributed by The Campanile Press, San Diego State University

Library of Congress Cataloging Data
Catalog Card No.: 77-83492
Stanford, E. Percil
The Elder Black
San Diego, Calif.: Campanile Press
p. 72
7708   770708

ISBN 0-916304-31-0

Distributed for the Center on Aging by
The Campanile Press
San Diego State University
5300 Campanile Drive
San Diego, California
92182

/E. P. Stanford

Acknowledgments

The black elderly are very special people who have been responsible for inspiring the younger black generations to live full and meaningful lives. It is because of that inspiration that many black elderly project a positive attitude about life, although they often live in environments considered to be undesirable by most. There is a direct relationship to the general spirit and will of the black elderly and the manner in which they gave freely of their time and energy to make this study a success. Without the cooperation and desire of the elderly to bring about a better quality of life for themselves, it would be impossible to present this material. The black elderly who participated cannot be given enough praise and thanks for their openness and willingness to share a most valuable possession—life experience and knowledge.

Social scientists are continuing to learn the value of involving the practitioner and the layman in their work. Without them this study would not have been successful. At the very beginning, agency and organization representatives from the black community gave their advice and support for the study. Many persons who were not formally associated with organizations freely gave their opinions and ideas regarding the purpose and direction of the study. Their comments were comprehensive and played a major role in determining what substantive areas should be explored.

A very important aspect of any survey research is the interview process. Interviewers are the most important link between the researcher and those providing information (the sample). Interviewers for this section of the study were Ida Hoggard, Bernice Rollins, Monja Thornton and Anthony Morrell. Because of their dedication to the black community and black older people, they were able to assist in gathering valuable data. The interviewers served not only as interviewers, but also as interpreters of data. More than anyone else, they were in a position to expand on the data presented because of their familiarity with the environment and tone of responses of the respondents.

The tasks of collating and typing are thankless and most essential. Carol Bassett cannot be thanked enough for her assistance throughout the data processing stages of the study. Cynthia Wright, Alicia Krotky, Peggy King, and Patricia Murphy willingly gave unlimited clerical assistance which enabled the study to be completed within a reasonable timeframe. In general, the team which undertook the San Diego Cross-Cultural Study in Aging has been a tremendous source of support. The group has been thought-provoking and positively critical throughout the research process.

An enormous amount of time and effort was spent developing the general list of references and the annotated bibliography. David Kaplan and Medria Williams are responsible for compiling references in the annotated bibliography. Their willingness to share material which has been outstanding for this study has been commendable.

There are also a number of other persons who have had varying degrees of impact to the project as a whole from the proposal stage to the end. Dr. Gideon Horowitz was instrumental in developing the proposal for which initial funds were received. Dr. James Ajemian assumed the directorship for the project during its first year. Mr. Charles Martinez provided extremely helpful technical support throughout the process of the research, especially at the point of finalizing the monographs. Dr. Roger Cunniff, Mrs. Sharon Swinscoe and Gerald Thiebolt of The Campanile Press were most helpful in extending their assistance throughout the process of publishing this editorial serial of reports. The researchers are equally appreciative of the continual support from the Administration on Aging by Mr. David Dowd, Project Officer. We wish also to recognize the School of Social Work of San Diego State University under whose general auspices the study was conducted.

We are grateful to all of the above for their involvement in this research effort.

/E. P. Stanford|

Table of Contents

I. INTRODUCTION TO THE STUDY*

Research Objectives

This study of black elders was undertaken as an integral part of a larger Cross-Cultural Study of Minority Elders of San Diego County. The study as a whole, extended over a two-year period, 1974-1976, and was funded by the Administration on Aging. In addition to blacks, seven other populations of minority elders were encompassed within the research. These included, American Indian, Chinese, Guamanian, Japanese, Latino, Pilipino, and Samoan elders, age 50 years or more. While the age designation might appear somewhat arbitrary, the half-century mark in chronological age was seen as encompassing the concept of elder as denoted within the study.

The research was undertaken with three specific objectives in mind:

- First, to analyze characteristic lifestyles and customs, as well as the primary interactional networks of ethnic minority groups and in this case, especially those of black elders.
- Second, to explore and delineate the perceptions and viewpoints of the black elders toward formal programmatic assistance and human service networks with the overall intent of tracing, where possible, the interactions between the formal programs and the primary networks.
- Third, to test out a methodology appropriate to obtaining information about ethnic minority populations and specifically the elders of these populations.

To a large extent, the third objective guided the total study. From the standpoint of the researchers, the methodology to be utilized was deemed extremely critical to the actual information obtained. The rationale for giving priority consideration to the research approach was twofold. It was grounded first in the researchers' previous data-gathering experiences in their respective ethnic communities, both within and outside San Diego. These experiences had provided information about the importance of such factors as providing for community relations when engaged in ethnic minority survey research efforts with ethnic minority populations. The reasoning for this approach was also based on the call for fresh research approaches both from minority social scientists, Romano (1969), Vaca (1970), Hamilton (1973), Murase (1972), Takagi (1973), as well as from ethnic majority investigators, Clark and Anderson (1967), Blauner (1973), and Moore (1973).

Study Populations

A predominant theme within the above collectivity of social investigators is the call for the utilization of what Myers (1974) has termed unconventional research approaches which, in effect, blend traditional survey research techniques with newer considerations. A major step in the direction of this methodological approach was the determination to seek a purposive, rather than statistically

---

* This methodological statement is authored by a group of researchers at the Center on Aging. With minor variations, it appears as the introductory chapter to the monographs on elder blacks, Chinese, Guamanians, Pilipinos, and Samoans, in the series, A Cross-Cultural Study of Minority Elders in San Diego.

proportionate representation of the ethnic groups. The overriding research intent was to obtain representation of ethnic life process content within the larger San Diego environment.

The San Diego environment.

The study was conducted within the County of San Diego which is also designated as a Complete Standard Metropolitan Statistical Area (SMSA) within the Bureau of Census. The total SMSA encompasses approximately 4,296 square miles and an estimated 1.5 million persons. To the south, it borders Baja California and the Mexican city of Tijuana. Orange County forms the northern border to the SMSA with the Los Angeles metropolitan complex then being immediately adjacent. To a large extent San Diego forms the nexus of a well-traveled commercial corridor stretching some 200 miles from Los Angeles to Ensenada in Baja California.

The San Diego area has an extensive military complex which serves as a base of operations for the United States Navy in several capacities including port and air facilities. The SMSA has a highly urbanized core, but is equally highly suburban. At the same time, large portions of the County are rural and sparsely populated. For example, nineteen American Indian tribes reside in rural reservations in the SMSA. There is considerable agriculture in the area wherein large numbers of persons of Mexican and Pilipino backgrounds are employed. The North County area of San Diego contains smaller cities with concentrated mixes of urban and rural populations.

Elders in San Diego.

At the initiation of the study, the researchers had varying estimates of the elderly population of the SMSA and opted to utilize the San Diego County Area Agency on Aging, 1975 projections based on the age 60-plus population. Of the total San Diego population, 1.5 million, approximately 198,300 or 13.2 percent were designated as 60-plus years. (See Table 1)

Table   1

San Diego SMSA Age 60-Plus Population Estimates
$N = 1,500,000$

Population age	f	%
Under 60 years	1,302,000	86.8
Over 60 years	198,300	13.2

SOURCE: San Diego County Area Agency on Aging, formerly the Office of Senior Citizen Affairs, updated 1975 estimates.

Of these estimated 198,300 elderly, approximately 23,900 (11.9 percent) have been classified as ethnic-minority elders, age 60 years or more (see Table 2). It must be noted, though, that the data regarding the elderly in San Diego were representations of the best estimates and projections available at the point of conducting the research.

The data regarding the ethnic elderly have been found to be in disarray due to repeated undercounts and mislabeling of ethnicity (*Counting the Forgotten*, 1974).

Table 2
San Diego SMSA Age 60-Plus
Population Estimates By Ethnic Groups

Group	f	Percent of Total Age 60-Plus Population N = 198,300	Percent of Minority 60-Plus Population By Ethnic Minority Group n = 23,900*
Anglo/White	174,400	87.9	
Latino	14,900	7.5	62.3
Black	4,500	2.2	18.8
Pilipino	1,300	0.6	5.4
Japanese	700	0.4	2.9
American Indian	500	0.3	2.0
Chinese	300	0.2	1.4
Samoan	300	0.2	1.4
Guamanian	200	0.1	0.8
Other ethnic minorities not clearly designated	1,200	0.6	5.0

*NOTE: The Area Agency on Aging estimates of specific ethnic minority populations have been further updated with best estimates available from organizations serving each population.

As can be seen from Table 2, Latinos account for almost two-thirds (62.3 percent) of the estimated total group of minority group elderly in the San Diego area.

The black study population.

A cost analysis of available project funds and time, as well as the methodology to be utilized, indicated that a study population of approximately 600 total subjects would be feasible. In fact, 628 ethnic minority persons were interviewed. Table 3 summarizes the Cross-Cultural Study population by specific ethnic designation. The further heterogeneity of each specific minority group studied along with the principal findings are described within the series of monographs commissioned through the research project.

As can be seen, despite the fact that the black elderly comprise approximately 18.8 percent of all the estimated minority elderly in San Diego, they formed only 16.1 percent of the total study population.

Here again, the research intent intervened. To have proceeded with population sampling on a ratio or numerically proportionate basis would have meant that the Latino sample would have taken an undue amount of the study group's time, such as to preclude obtaining representative content from the other ethnic minorities.

The earlier noted disarray of demographic indicator on minority groups was also a contributing factor for the research decision to seek purposive representativeness.

Table   3

AoA Study Population

N = 628

Group	f	%
Latino	218	34.7
Black	101	16.1
Pilipino	74	11.8
American Indian	62	9.8
Japanese	60	9.6
Chinese	50	7.9
Samoan	40	6.4
Guamanian	23	3.7

The Cross-Cultural Research Group

Each ethnic minority group had a complement of university-based researchers who acted as coordinators and community-based interviewers in numbers adequate to the size of the ethnic cohort included in the study. A research decision appropriate to the methodology had indicated that researchers of the same ethnicity would operate within their respective cohorts. This strategy permitted the tailoring of the research instruments and contact patterns specifically to the linguistic and situational differentials to be encountered within each ethnic cohort. Specifically this approach allowed the translation of the interview guides into the idiom appropriate to the ethnic group to be studied.

Fortunately, the concept of providing for a match between the ethnicity of the researcher and study population had been built into the original proposal and budget, although, not in the fineline detail as necessitated at the point of actual implementation. In its totality, the research group numbered ten university-based and twenty-eight community-based interviewers who had the support of one full-time technical assistant and three clerical staff.

II. METHODOLOGY

Overview

The research strategy utilized within the inquiry was based on the theoretical perspective of combining quantitative and qualitative research approaches so that the information obtained from close-ended questions would be placed in the context of the social environment of the respondent. The theoretical sets utilized in the research stem from Glazer and Strauss (1967), Campbell and Stanley (1963), Gouldner (1965), and Sieber (1973), who collectively propose alternative considerations for survey research. In addition, the direction for the research was drawn from Myers (1974) and Valle (1974), whose empirical research demonstrated approaches toward combining both quantitative and qualitative analysis.

Figure 1 highlights the data collection strategy. If the research approach could be summarized, it could be said to have been geared to the collection of what Cooley (1908) and other theorists have termed primary group behaviors against the backdrop of complex secondary social environments. With regard to the San Diego SMSA, these include mixes of ethnically different populations living in urbanized as well as dispersed and ruralized situations and all living in an equally complex network of systems and services. The questions asked by the researchers centered then both on obtaining indicators of ethnicity and primary behaviors in the context of their secondary group and interactional environments.

Figure 1
Overall Strategy for Data Collection

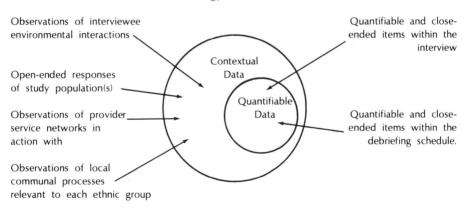

In operational terms, the methodology deployed within the study encompassed a series of lockstep phases and planned sequential interactions beginning with community involvement.

Community Consultation and Dissemination Network

A key ingredient to the total research effort was the development and maintenance of a multilevel pattern of interaction with varied constituencies from each of the ethnic minority groups throughout the life of the study. To some extent, the rationale for this mode also arose from the expressed reluctance early in 1974 of various minority constituencies to have more university researchers traipsing through their communities, even though the researchers might be ethnics themselves. This process though, had been anticipated by the researchers before word of the proposed research was allowed to circulate throughout the broader community.

In setting up the contact network, each coordinator was made responsible for the formal and informal interfacing with his or her ethnic group constituencies. The process was designed to be continuously open throughout the life of the study. It was expected that some of the constituencies would not or could not become involved at the beginning of the process. Either some constituencies were unknown to the researchers, or they would not become informed until sometime after the project was well underway. In this manner, any of the constituent groups desiring information and access to the research could secure what was available at whatever point in time they entered the process.

It should be noted that as time permitted, a like pattern of open interaction was maintained with constituencies other than the ethnic minorities and included other researchers, both within San Diego and in other cities, to include persons significantly involved in the field of aging.

As envisioned by the researchers, the benefits of this process far outweighed the time expenditure drawbacks in that the continuous interaction facilitated obtaining of the project interviewers as well as the study subjects. Moreover, the maintenance of this ongoing contact has, at the point of termination of the project, provided the project with a built-in dissemination network of interested individuals who could directly address the findings of the inquiry. In keeping with this intent, each of the research coordinators filed his or her dissemination plan at the end of the project, in order to coordinate dissemination activity beyond the expiration of project funds.

Population Selection

The study cohort was selected on the basis of attempting to tap into the normal or ordinary relational patterns of the ethnic populations targeted to be included within the study. Initial selection was therefore based on lists of potential respondents obtained from the several constituencies to which the researchers were already linked. In many instances, this meant that the initial selection included a number of persons who formally belonged to ethnic organizations. From that point, allowance was made for individuals to be included in the study on the basis of referrals from some of the interviewees themselves, as well as from other community persons, once the interviewer had obtained credibility either in a particular neighborhood or interactional linkage network. With conscious intent, the population selection process was designed to include brokering persons who often served as connectors between the interviewer and the potential interviewee. These brokering or contact persons could be translators, community volunteers or agency workers, or simply key neighborhood leaders.

Interviewer Selection and Training

The community consultation process as designed also provided the vehicle whereby the university-based researchers could obtain a cadre of potential interviewers. The ongoing contact with the community was such as to allow both the university-based researchers and prospective community-based interviewers to prescreen each other. In practice, the four-month period of November 1974 through to February 1975, was allotted to this purpose. As a consequence, when the training period began in March of 1975, a preselected group of interviewers was available from all of the respective ethnic groups.

The formal training for the interviewers encompassed twenty-eight hours. The interviewers were trained both as a total group and within their respective ethnic group where individualized concerns about language, customs, and interview style were emphasized. The first two interviews per interviewer were made part of the training process and all interviewers were debriefed intensively to reinforce the training as to fine tune the methodology.

Throughout the training, the interviewers were encouraged to proceed with their own natural styles. It should be noted that the community interaction had acted as a screening process and had attracted individuals who were experienced either as volunteers or agency aides. In some instances, several came to the study with prior formal research interviewing experience on other projects. The overall training intent was to free the interviewers to augment their own natural and culturally appropriate capabilities while at the same time, furnishing them with the necessary data collection and recording techniques.

In the second year of the project, the interviewers were invited to join in the analysis, as well as participate in the documentation of the findings in a continued part-time paid capacity. The interviewers also joined in the dissemination efforts of the project.

Interview Strategy

The *plática* research methodology (Valle, 1974), combined with the "unconventional survey research approach," (Myers, 1974), as utilized throughout the total study has several distinguishing features. First, the interview is seen as an interaction which has all the trappings of a beginning interpersonal relationship (Stebbins, 1972). Second, the strategy builds upon an open discussion approach wherein the interview proceeds in the format of building trust and confidence on a conversational and mutual exchange basis. Third, within this kind of interviewing, the research focus is first on all of the human exchange aspects and only then on the information to be obtained. Fourth, the maintenance of the relationship-oriented conversational approach is seen as continuous throughout the total interview. Fifth, the strategy includes the incorporation of observational techniques (Sieber, 1972), wherein the interviewer observes the living surroundings and environmental interactions of the interviewee. By design the interviews were seen as taking place in the interviewee's home. Sixth, at all points of the interview, the interviewer secures the consent of the interviewee to obtain information on an ongoing basis as appropriate throughout the interview process. The interviewer is mandated to be especially sensitive to obtain consent to more sensitive personal information areas and to provide the option to the interviewee either to refuse to answer or to terminate the interview. The culturally syntonic (appropriate) clues, both verbal and affective, which comprise the core of this approach were worked out in the training period, as well as in the debriefing.

With regard to the notion of informed consent, it should be noted that the study was initiated prior to the promulgation of the Department of Health, Education, and Welfare human subject research guidelines *Federal Register* (1975). The informed consent procedures utilized within the study did conform to the option of modified procedures wherein the written consent of the interviewee is not required but respondent's rights to privacy and refusal to participate are clearly protected. The best advice of the project's community consultants and interviewers had indicated that the Guamanian elders' apprehension might well be increased rather than decreased by having to sign consent forms.

The Interview Instrument

The interview instrument was designed to be utilized as a guide for information collection within specific categories. This approach was selected on the basis of the diversity of the languages (and dialects) represented within the study populations. For example, the Chinese population group represented a number of the Chinese dialects, to include, Cantonese and Mandarin. Within the Pilipino group, several provincial languages were represented, including Tagalog and Ilocano. In practice, this meant that the field researchers utilized a basic interview instrument containing questions grouped around sixteen major variable categories congruent with the stated research objectives of the inquiry.

An illustration might assist in clarifying the instrument design. A key item of information for the study was obtaining the respondent's age. Among some of the ethnic groups, Latinos and Japanese in particular, it is culturally rude to ask another's age directly. More circumspect behaviors are required, for example, first obtaining the place of birth and then requesting permission to record the date. This meant also that in some cases, the dates were provided in terms of other than the Occidental calendar. In these instances, the responses were given in terms of significant events which had taken place within the ethnic minority group history. For example, being born at the point of a major immigration by a whole village to the United States. The selection of interviewers then focused on their ability to move easily between the standard interview data to be obtained and the cultural nuances attendant to the interviewee's ethnically-based responses.

In keeping with the contextual strategy of the research, the instrument contained open-ended items woven in between the close-ended questions. The interviewer often then had to phrase all of these questions in the particular local idiom. Overall, the interview was designed to be a relatively long interpersonal experience. Moveover, it was approached from the aspect that it could be a pleasant and possibly therapeutic experience for the respondent.

Data Collection Procedures

Data collection included three distinct operations: the interview itself, recording of the data and debriefing.

The interview process.

While variations in the interview style were allowed, a general pattern was established in training. This involved developing a set of interview behaviors deemed appropriate, such as establishing precontacts in the mode acceptable to specific ethnic groups. These precontacts could range from a written letter or a phone call through to having a cultural broker intercede in order to establish the interview. During the interview itself, the field researchers were free to accept food and drink as deemed appropriate and to vary the interview length and intensity also as appropriate. By predetermination, all interviewees were paid an honorarium of ten dollars for their time and effort, regardless of length or completeness of the interview. The honorarium was not announced beforehand, but provided at the end of the interview. The rationale for the payment to interviewees emerged from the several ethnic constituencies whose members were advising the research project. In their collective thinking the ten dollars represented an in-kind exchange to the interviewee for his or her time and information.

Data collection.

Data was collected at all points of the interview. The interviewers were encouraged to record open-ended responses in as much detail as possible and in the language of the respondents. The interviewers also were equally encouraged to record any open-ended additions given in the context of any close-ended item, as it would be elicited in the course of the interview. A common illustration might serve to highlight the process. In many instances, the above-noted request for the close-ended date of birth would often elicit open-ended discussion around the early life experiences of the respondent.

In terms of recording style, the interviewers were left free to record information during the interview and/or after the interview itself, depending on respondent's comfortableness with the situation, as well as depending upon the procedures as acceptable by each ethnic group. This approach was also designed to accommodate the information storage style of the interviewer. Some were more comfortable writing during the interview, some more so immediately after. A general capability among the interviewer group was their skill in the area of retaining and reporting back oral history-type process which was tested out during the training stage of the research.

Debriefing.

In the actual working out of the research, the interviewers were debriefed according to various modes. These included debriefings on an interview by interview basis, as well as debriefings encompassing the interviewer's total sample. The debriefing intent was to collect as much contextual data regarding each interview as possible as well as to obtain as much descriptive information surrounding what might be considered the more open-ended items within the guide. Debriefings were conducted by the university-based coordinators. A debriefing schedule complete with close-ended coded items was developed for the research.

Data Analysis

The analysis of the data was seen as a mesh of both quantitative and qualitative approaches. With regard to the quantitative data, the Statistical Package for Social Sciences (SPSS) computer program format was employed. For the purposes of the monograph level of reporting, frequency distributions and percentages were seen as the most appropriate statistical format. For purposes of the major project report which compares intergroup variables, statistical measures including analysis of variance and factor analysis were seen as applicable. In all instances, the quantitative analysis was to be played against the backdrop of the ethnic-environmental context in which it was obtained.

The process of analysis was seen as being relatively long in duration, consuming most of the second year of the project. During this phase, the interviewers joined the university-based researchers as fellow analysts and assisted in conceptualizing and interpreting the findings, as well as in instances, assisting in writing portions of the final monograph products.

Expected Outcomes

The expected outcomes of the research were cast in terms of the three principal study objectives: to trace the respective cultural patterns of the ethnically varied study population; to delineate the respondents' outlooks toward formal services and networks of services; and to test an alternative data gathering methodology.

It was expected that the study, as a whole, including this series of monographs, would provide findings to impact the field of aging at four levels: (a) with regard to direct services and programs for ethnic elders, (b) with regard to policies affecting minority seniors, (c) with regard to the training of professionals to serve in the field of aging, and (d) with regard to further research in the field of ethnicity and aging.

Methodological Considerations Specific to the Black Sample

The interviewers were instructed to make precontact by telephone or in person in order to establish their credibility and to identify themselves. In most instances, telephone calls were made prior to going out to talk with individuals. There were situations where face-to-face meeting took place to establish a future time for interviews. The percentages given subsequently reflect the number of precontacts made in person. It was found that 17.8 percent had no previous contacts in person, 77.2 percent had one precontact, 4.0 percent two precontacts and 1.0 percent had three or more. Those precontacted by telephone outnumbered those who required in-person contacts. Of the total sample, 68.3 percent required one telephone precontact, 3 percent required two such precontacts, 1.0 percent required three or more telephone precontacts and 27.7 percent required no precontacts by phone. Only one person was precontacted by letter.

All interviews were taken in English. Interviewers reported little or no difficulty in understanding the interviewees. In one or two instances persons were very old, somewhat ill and had difficulty enunciating. However, that was not a language problem. The older black respondents, unlike their cohorts in other ethnic-cultural groups, have the advantage of understanding and being able to operationally use the English language.

Considerable time and care was given to outline the reasonable or appropriate manner in which to go into the black community to acquire information. It was understood that many black older persons had recently gone through a series of extensive interviews by other organizations gathering data. Consideration was given to whether young, older, females, or males should go into the community to elicit the cooperation of the older potential respondent. After considerable thought, the decision was made to involve as many older black women as possible in the interview process. The decision to use these individuals was made primarily because of the ease with which they may be accepted in the community. It was anticipated that most persons to be interviewed would be women and that they would probably more readily accept older women into their homes than younger women, or men—younger or older.

Another very important consideration was that the older black woman is the person who is generally available and responds to the needs of those persons who need help in the community. Therefore, she is the one who most naturally has entry into homes of her peers or others in the community.

The significance of using agency personnel to initially discuss approaches to be used in gathering data was that they might have known reasons why the researchers should not be asking certain types of questions. In addition, many agency personnel could supplement the interview process by advising the researchers on questions and problems that would be useful for themselves in the future.

Nationally, the number of black elderly has risen from 1.2 million in 1960 to 1.6 million in 1970. They now constitute 7.8 percent of the total black population. Black people have a lower life expectancy than whites, resulting, we can safely assume, from the generally lower socioeconomic status accorded to blacks in the United States. (Butler, 1973.)

Southeast San Diego with a population of about 55,000 extends over a huge area, some 5,000 acres, and is anything but a compact community. The aging make up 10.9 percent of the total population in the area. The community is torn apart by freeways; buildings are clustered among vast vacant spaces; and some three-hundred acres are occupied by cemetaries. It is difficult, even using private cars, to get from one area to another; nothing seems within walking distance and public transportation is inadequate and inconvenient.

III. FINDINGS

This section includes a presentation of findings from the sample of black older people interviewed. The findings will be presented on several topical and subtopical areas, and are based on the content areas covered by the interview guide. In the conventional style of interviewing adopted by this research, the interviewee was not required to give responses to all questions asked. For varied reasons, some interviewees chose not to respond to some questions, therefore, the percentages used in this report are based on the number of responses to any given question.

A Profile of the Black Study Group

Age and sex distribution.

The sample consisted of 101 older black persons. There were 43 males (42.6 percent) and 58 females (57.4 percent) with an age range from 52 through 95. The mean age was 70.6 years. Unlike most of the other cultural groups in the study, all of the black older persons were native born and each spoke English as the primary language.

Education.

The importance given to education was quite obvious in discussions with respondents of the sample. Respondents who went to school were 89.1 percent versus 7.9 percent not attending. Of those attending, 3.0 percent said that they were self-educated. The mean number of years of formal education for the sample was 8.9 years and the maximum number of years of education was 20. Those receiving from 1—5 years were 27.7 percent; 6—10 years, 44.6 percent; and 11—20 years, 24.8 percent with 2.9 percent receiving no formal education. The breakdown for elementary school (1—8 years) was 47.5 percent, high school (9—12 years) 41.6 percent and college/vocational, 8.0 percent.

Employment.

The number of respondents currently working was 11.9 percent, with 83.2 percent not working and 4.9 percent indicating not applicable. Those who had spouses working numbered 8.9 percent, while 36.6 percent did not have working spouses and 54.5 percent indicated not applicable. Six percent of the respondents were working full time and 6.9 percent were working part time. Of the spouses working, 5 percent were working full time and 5 percent working part time, with 90.1 percent indicating not applicable (Figure 2).

In order to get an idea of the work history of the respondents, they were asked if they had worked in the past (see Figure 3). Of those responding, 94.1 percent indicated that they had and 4.0 percent said they had not. The same question was asked regarding the work history of spouses; 51.5 percent responsed positively and 2.0 percent responded negatively. To get a further understanding of the past work involvement, respondents were asked to indicate the length of time they had not been working. Five percent indicated less than one year, 9.9 percent, 1-2 years; 11.9 percent, 2 years or more but less than 5 years; and 60.4 percent, 5-10 years.

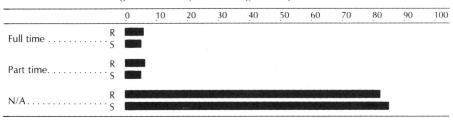

Figure 2. Are you working full or part time?

Key: R = Respondent
S = Spouse

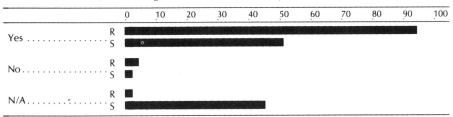

Figure 3. Worked in the past?

Key: R = Respondent
S = Spouse

Of those spouses currently not working, 24.8 percent had not worked from 5-10 years; 3 percent from less than 5 years but more than 2; 2 percent had not been working from 1-2 years; and 1 percent had been working less than one year.

Income.

Participants in the study were asked to rate their financial situations. The majority of the respondents rated their financial situations as "fair," which amounted to 57.4 percent. At the same time, 15.8 percent indicated that their financial situation was "good" compared to 25.7 percent rating their financial situation as "poor." The mean monthly income for the sample was $299.98, with a maximum of $1,000 per month. Individuals receiving from 0-$200 per month represented 19.9 percent, and those earning over $430, 14.0 percent. Sources of income came from Social Security, wages/salaries, Department of Welfare/SSI, and a variety of pensions and insurances. The percentages of persons receiving funds from the aforementioned categories were 79.2 percent, 5.0 percent, and 3.0 percent respectively, with 2.8 percent showing other resources.

About one-fifth of the respondents (20.9 percent) reported receiving a monthly average income from $209 to $250 and 26.8 percent said they received from $252 to $300 per month. As many as 35.9 percent received $334 per month.

Since many older people have no ready source of income for emergencies, most need assistance periodically. The respondents were asked to whom they turn for minor financial help, as well as major financial help. They indicated that they depended on themselves, family members, or friends in most instances. For minor financial help the first priority ranking was no one or self, 9.9 percent; family member, 57.4 percent; friend, 25.7 percent; agency or professional person, 1.0 percent; and member of an organized group, 2.0 percent. The first priority listing for major financial help showed no one or self, 12.9 percent; family member, 46.5 percent; friend, 27.7 percent; agency or professional person, 4.0 percent; and member of an organized group, 1.0 percent.

Origins and residency patterns.

Residency was an important factor in looking at lifestyles of the older black persons. The data showed 28.2 years as the mean for number of years lived in San Diego, with 73.0 years being the maximum (range = 1-73). The mean number of years in the same place was 15.9 years with a maximum of 50.0 and a minimum of 0.0. Many of the older people owned their own homes (41.6 percent), while 46.5 percent rented and 8.0 percent living with others or not paying for lodging.

Repairs on housing are very expensive and also difficult to accomplish. Respondents gave a clear indication of the problem in that 48.5 percent, 8.9 percent and 6.9 percent respectively said they get repairs without difficulty, with some difficulty and it is almost impossible to get repairs, with 35.6 percent indicating not applicable.

Despite the difficulty of upkeep and repairs, the monthly payments are somewhat high. The monthly payment scale is: less than $50, 2 percent; $50-59, 43.6 percent; $100-149, 18.8 percent; $150-199, 3.0 percent; $200-249, 1 percent; $250-299, 1 percent and 30.7 percent not applicable.

Many of the older persons had lived in their home or apartment for several years. Those living in their home or apartment one year or less was 9.9 percent; 1-5 years, 20.8 percent; 6-10 years, 20.8 percent; 11-20 years, 26.7 percent; 20 plus years, 21.8 percent and the average time in a house or apartment was 10 plus years. When asked if they would move, 30.7 percent said yes and 65.3 percent said no with 4 percent indicating not applicable. (See Figure 4.)

Figure 4.   Would you move if you could?

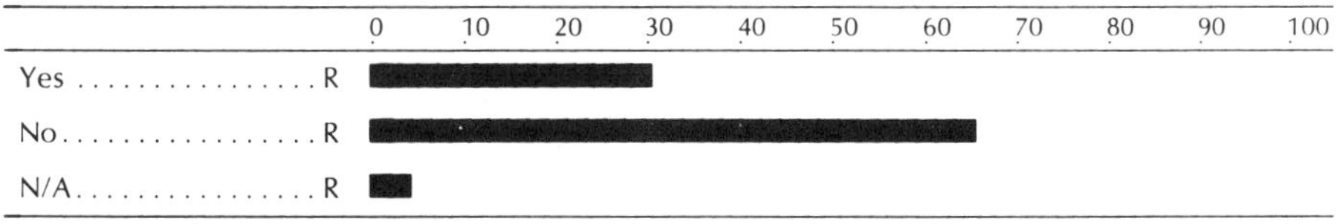

	0	10	20	30	40	50	60	70	80	90	100
Yes . . . . R											
No . . . . R											
N/A . . . . R											

Key: R = Respondent

Expressed Needs

Health.

Respondents were asked to give their opinion of their health status. Only 27.7 percent felt that they had "good" health; 17.8 percent felt that their health was "poor," another 53.5 percent responded "fair," and 1 percent indicated not applicable. Respondents were also given an opportunity to develop three sets of priorities for getting support for themselves when becoming ill. They were asked the question, "To whom do you turn in the time of sickness?" Their first set of priorities was self or no one, family member, friend, neighbor, agency/professional person, or member of an organized group. The responses for the foregoing categories were 5.0 percent, 63.4 percent, 18.8 percent, 1.0 percent, 7.9 percent, 2.0 percent respectively and 2.0 percent shown as "other." In a second set of priorities, they listed family member, friend, neighbor, agency/professional person, or member of an organized group. The respective percentages to those responding were 3.0 percent, 15.8 percent, 5.9 percent, 1.0 percent, 2.0 percent, with 2.0 percent indicating "other" and 7.03 percent saying not applicable. The third set of priorities developed with family member being first succeeded by agency/professional person and member of an organized group with the respective percentages of 1.0 percent, 5.0 percent, 2.0 percent and 1.0 percent; with 1 percent saying "don't know," and 90.1 percent indicating not applicable.

Many black older people have never been residents in nursing homes, convalescent hospitals or midway facilities. Of the participants in this study, 52.5 percent have been in hospitals, nursing homes or similar insitutions, while 41.6 percent said they had not, and 6 percent said not applicable.

Many older people did not seek the care of hospital staff, doctors or other professionals in the medical field. Respondents were asked why they do not go to those who can provide professional medical services. Respondents were given an opportunity to list their rationale for not going to the hospital or doctor in three priority categories. The first priority category was language (5 percent); financial obligation too great (9.9 percent); mistrust or no faith (14.8 percent); fear of illness and the consequences (52.5 percent); transportation (4.0 percent); and inconvenience (2.0 percent), with the categories of other and not applicable being 5.9 percent each. The second category had fear of illness and mistrust (11.9 percent each) as primary reasons for not going to a professional medical person and the third category had finances as number one (6.9 percent).

Transportation.

The respondents were asked to indicate their primary means of transportation and to prioritize the various means into three categories. The responses for the first priority ranking were: 4.0 percent, walking; 49.5 percent, automobile; 41.6 percent, public transportation (bus); with 4 percent and 1 percent being shown as other and not applicable. The second priority ranking was 11.9 percent, walking; 17.8 percent, automobile; 21.8 percent, public transportation (bus); with 37.6 percent and 10.9 percent indicating other and not applicable. The third showed 14.9 percent, walking; 9.9 percent, automobile; 16.8 percent, public transportation (bus); 42.6 percent other and not applicable, 15.8 percent.

The respondents were also asked to indicate whose automobile was used when a private auto was taken. Their responses showed that 39.6 percent said that they owned a car; 1.0 percent borrowed an automobile; 39.6 percent said that someone else drove, and 19.8 percent indicated not applicable.

Generally, most of the black older people indicated that transportation is usually available. The percentage responding positively was 88.1 percent and the percentage responding negatively was 11.9 percent.

"To whom do you turn for transportation?" was asked of the respondents. The responses in a first priority ranking were as follows: 5.9 percent said self or no one; 43.6 percent, family member; 29.7 percent, friend; 5.0 percent, neighbor; 5.0 percent, agency/professional person; 1.0 percent, member of an organized group; other, 6.9 percent; and 3.0 percent, not applicable.

Nutrition.

The eating habits of black older people have been described as being unique and different, particularly when compared to the Anglo population. Respondents, in conversation, as well as through implication of the data do not appear to have eating habits extensively different from those of the Anglo cohorts. The highest percentage of respondents ate two meals a day (57.4 percent), while 35.6 percent ate three meals per day and 6.9 percent had only one meal per day (Figure 5). The typical diet for most people (63.5 percent), was mixed ethnic food or non-ethnic food, while 27.7 percent indicated that they had what they would consider mostly an ethnic diet, 7.9 percent said their diet was mostly non-ethnic, and 1.0 percent said it was not applicable (Figure 6).

Figure 5. Number of meals per day

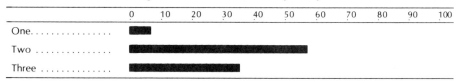

Figure 6. Type of meals on a typical day

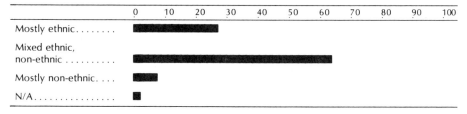

Eating alone seems to be the characteristic of most of the black older people. Reasons for eating alone could be explained due to the high percentage of widows in the sample. Actually, 40.6 percent of the black older respondents ate alone; 36.6 percent ate with one other person; 18.8 percent had meals with two to four persons; 2.0 percent had meals with five to nine others; and 2.0

percent had meals with ten or more people. The significance of the high number of other persons eating meals with respondents is that many are eating in congregate meal settings. Only a few are living in situations where they would be expected or required to eat with several other persons (Figure 7).

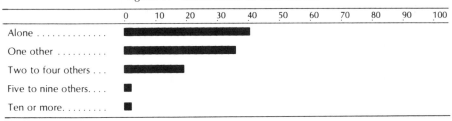

Figure 7. Meals alone or with others?

Since most of the persons responding lived alone, 69.3 percent prepared their own meals and 10.9 percent had spouses who prepared meals. An adult from the neighborhood or a relative prepared meals for 8.9 percent; children under 21 fixed meals for 1.0 percent; 5.0 percent had a housekeeper to prepare meals; 3.0 percent went to a community central nutrition site for meals and 2.0 percent had a variety of arrangements (Figure 8). Many older people must have special diets for health reasons. It was shown that 27.7 percent of the sample of black older persons must have special diets and 1.0 percent said that they did not. The interesting and perhaps the significant finding is that 71.3 percent indicated that it was not applicable or was of no concern to them.

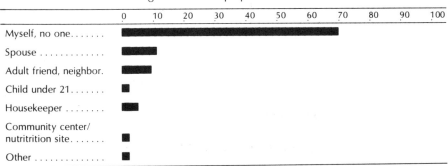

Figure 8. Who prepares meals?

Considerable attention has been given to ways in which meal times can be more pleasurable and beneficial to older persons beyond the nutritional value. The respondents were asked to indicate ways in which their meal times can be improved. They were asked to rank order of several areas in priority categories. The first category rank ordering was: 12.9 percent, more variety; 9.9 percent, more companionship; 2.0 percent, more food; 1.0 percent, better quality food; 1.0 percent, ethnic food; 1.0 percent, food program; 68.3 percent felt it was not applicable and 4.0 percent felt that there were other ways meals could be improved, but did not elaborate.

There are many times when older persons who are dependent upon pensions of a limited nature or other limited fixed incomes do not have adequate resources for the purchase of food. Many ethnic older people have been supported by friends, family relatives, or neighbors in these situations. Respondents were asked to prioritize in rank order the persons or individuals to whom they turn when they need food. The first ranking included yourself or no one (7.9 percent); family member (55.4 percent); friend (24.8 percent); neighbor (2.0 percent); agency/professional person (2.0 percent); other avenues (5.9 percent); and not applicable (2.0 percent).

Coping Patterns and Respondent Network

Interactional and coping patterns.

Ninety and one-tenth (90.1) percent said, yes, they have family, while 9.9 percent did not. Respondents were asked if they had brothers, sisters, children, grand-or great-grandchildren, parents or others in the same residence. Their respective responses were 3.0 percent, 7.9 percent, 5.9 percent, 2.0 percent, 2.0 percent saying "yes" and 97.0 percent, 94.1 percent, 98.0 percent and 98.0 percent saying "no." When asked if they had brothers or sisters in the immediate neighborhood, the county of San Diego or outside the county, 5.9 percent, 18.8 percent and 41.6 percent respectively said "yes." Respondents having children in the neighborhood, San Diego County or outside the county were 10.9 percent, 34.7 percent, and 28.7 percent respectively, and those with parents in the same area responded positively in the following sequence: 2.0 percent; 1.0 percent; 0.0 percent; and 7.9 percent.

The positive response to having grand or great-grandchildren in the neighborhood, San Diego County or outside San Diego County was: 11.9 percent, 26.7 percent, and 20.8 percent respectively (see Table 4).

Table   4

Location of Family $n = 101$

(Responses herein include only those saying "yes")

	Brothers/ Sisters (%)	Children (%)	Grand Child/ Great-Grand- Children (%)	Parents (%)	Others (%)
Same residence	3.0	7.9	5.9	2.0	2.0
Immediate Neighborhood	5.9	10.9	11.9	1.0	0.0
S.D. County	18.8	34.7	26.7	0.0	3.0
Outside S.D. County	41.6	28.7	20.8	7.9	5.0
N/A	38.6	27.7	41.6	88.1	92.1

Respondents were asked to indicate the frequency of contact with relatives. The response showed 4.0 percent as never having contact with relatives. Further, when asked about contact on a daily, weekly or more often, at least monthly, at least yearly, or less than a year basis, the number responding to the aforementioned categories was 12.9 percent, 35.6 percent, 12.9 percent, 13.9 percent, 11.9 percent, respectively, with 8.9 percent indicating not applicable.

Respondents indicated that they did not get together more often for the following reasons: distance (53.4 percent); transportation (3.0 percent); legal status (1.0 percent); time (3.0 percent); and relational problems (2.0 percent), with "other" 11.9 percent and 25.8 percent indicating not applicable. Respondents were asked to give second and third priority for not getting together. Transportation was listed as highest, as a second priority (14.9 percent) and also highest for the third priority (1.0 percent).

It is often assumed that older people want to be with family and relatives more often. To examine that assumption, participants in the study were asked to indicate the degree to which they would like to have contact with family. Forty-four and six tenths (44.6) percent indicated they would like to get together more often, while 45.5 percent said about the same and 1.0 percent said they would like to have contact with family less often, and 8.9 percent shown as not applicable.

When difficulties arise, many individuals seek out professional or public service assistance. Many older people continue to rely on family or those persons who live very close to them. The percentage of persons going to public agencies for assistance is quite low. Family member, no one, neighbor, friend, social agency, priest, and others were the categories to which respondents could relate. Responses were: 46.5 percent, 5.0 percent, 4.0 percent, 12.9 percent, 12.9 percent, 2.0 percent and 4.0 percent respectively to the aforementioned categories. The percentage indicating don't know or not applicable were 1.0 percent and 11.7 percent respectively.

Helping patterns.

Since the black older person has been as one who does not take advantage of public agencies, but receives help from friends, neighbors, and relatives, it is of interest to determine the extent to which they help others. Positive responses to the question, "Do you help others?" were given by 69.3 percent, and negative responses were given by 30.7 percent. To follow-up on that question, respondents were asked how often, and 26.7 percent said often, 21.8 percent indicated sometime, 30.7 percent said very little, and 20.8 percent indicated not applicable. The respondents prioritize the persons or groups that they help. The first priority ranking for the black older persons was friend/neighbor (54.5 percent); family (8.9 percent); church or church members (5.5 percent); member of organized groups (4.0 percent); other (3 percent); don't know (1 percent), and 23.8 percent felt that the question was not applicable.

The kind of help given is rather variable. The help given most often was in the area of physical help or normal chores (19.8 percent); sickness (16.8 percent); transportation (10.9 percent); financial (12.9 percent); food/meals (1.0 percent); talking/counseling (4 percent); don't know (9.9 percent); and not applicable (23.8 percent). The categorical rankings in the second and third priority listings are similar to the first priority given above with very little variance.

Relationship to Formal Services

MediCal and Medicare are very important to older people in our society. However, many do not take advantage of the public medical assistance programs. Respondents were asked if they knew about MediCal and Medicare. Ninety-eight percent said yes, they knew about MediCal and 92.1 percent responded positively about Medicare. At the same time, 2 percent said they did not know about MediCal and 7.9 percent said that they did not know about Medicare. Many knew about MediCal and Medicare but 74.3 percent said that they actually used MediCal, with 66.3 percent actually using Medicare. On the other hand, 25.7 percent said that they did not use MediCal and 33.7 percent said that they did not use Medicare.

Services.

To the question, "Can you think of any kind of help which, to your knowledge, is not available, but you think is needed, either by yourself or other older people?" participants prioritized their responses in three categories. The first category shows more social service programs (30.7 percent); jobs (3.0 percent); other (5.9 percent); I don't know (2.0 percent); not applicable (58.4 percent). The second category shows more social programs (5.0 percent); out-reach programs (2.0 percent); I don't know (2.0 percent); not applicable (91.0 percent). The third priority listing shows 2.0 percent indicating they do not know and 98.0 percent saying it is not applicable. Agency workers very often are not aware of ways in which they can improve services to older clients. The question, "Can you think of any specific things that agency workers providing services should know or be aware of that would help provide better services?" was asked. A positive response was given by 20.8 percent and a negative response was given by 79.2 percent. It was thought that a very much higher percentage would have had some very specific things to suggest to service providers. The responses given above correspond somewhat to the responses given when asked if formal agencies or service organizations were helping to meet needs. Those indicating yes were 75.2 percent and those saying no were 24.8 percent. Some respondents felt that agency personnel knew their needs (14.9 percent); personnel are courteous and patient (2.0 percent); 2.0 percent indicated other and 81.2 percent felt that it was not applicable.

Agencies help to meet only some of the needs of ethnic older people. More of the needs of black older people are met by formal agencies. Respondents indicated their use of a variety of agencies for particular services. The responses were prioritized categorically. The first priority ranking of the older black persons was health/medical care (61.4 percent); finance (4.0 percent); nutrition (14.9 percent); transportation (14.9 percent); legal aid (1.0 percent); other (3 percent); and 4.0 percent do not know, with 10.9 percent indicating that agency help is not applicable. The priority listings for each of the three priority areas have the categories ranked virtually in the same order as shown above. In order to pursue the idea of agency use, respondents were asked if they actually use any formal agency. Those having used or currently using were 49.5 percent, those who would use were 37.6 percent, and those indicating that they would not use a formal agency was 1.0 percent. Another 8.9 percent said they did not feel it was a meaningful question and another 3.0 percent said they really did not know.

Aspects of Life Satisfaction

Immediate living environment.

The attitudes of older persons about their neighborhood is significant when planning for delivery of services or the types of services to be delivered. The following findings provide meaningful insights into the outlook of some of the older people regarding their community: 41.6 percent felt that their neighborhood was "good," while 45.5 percent and 10.9 percent respectively felt that their neighborhood was "fair" or "poor," with 1 percent saying don't know and 1 percent saying not applicable (Figure 9). There was some indication that there were some positive points about the neighborhood. Some of the most important reasons were that they would be near their family, they had good neighbors, they were close to necessary resources, there was a degree of comfortableness, and they were long-time residents and owned their own home. The percentage of persons responding in the aforementioned manner was: 17.8 percent, 51.5 percent, 5.9 percent, 6.9 percent, 2.0 percent respectively with 2.0 percent and 13.9 percent respectively indicating other and not applicable (Figure 10). As a second priority, 11.9 percent indicated convenience to resources, 14.9 percent said comfortable and secure, 6.9 percent said long-time residents and owned own home; 1.0 percent relished their independence; 3 percent said other and 47.5 percent said not applicable. Generally, a smaller percentage (2.0 percent, 5.0 percent and 2.0 percent) said that they liked the neighborhood because people were good neighbors, the ethnicity of the neighborhood and its convenience to resources was a third set of priorities.

Of respondents who disliked their neighborhood, 12.9 percent said they just don't like the neighborhood, while 2.0 percent, 4.0 percent and 14.9 percent respectively, gave reasons such as no family, inconveniences and lack of resources, and lack of security and high crime with 16.8 percent indicating other and 49.5 percent saying not applicable (Figure 11). In a second category, 4.0 percent indicated they did not like their neighborhood; 2.0 percent indicated no friends; 3.0 percent said lack of security and high crime; 1 percent said other, and 90.1 percent said not applicable.

Figure 9. Respondents' opinion of their neighborhood

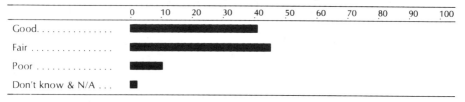

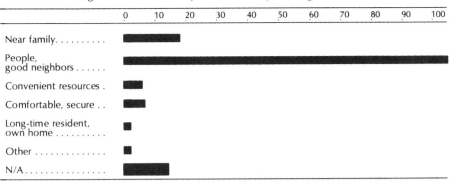

Figure 10. What do you like about your neighborhood?

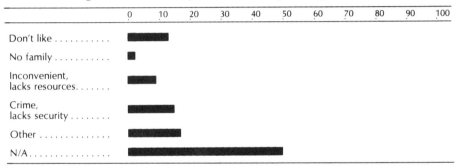

Figure 11. What do you dislike about your neighborhood?

Activities

Isolation is one of the greatest fears of persons who are in the process of aging. Too often, older people do not have cohorts to associate with on a daily basis. Respondents in this study were asked to prioritize their activities. Each respondent had four choices: alone, with family, with friends, or with organized groups. The highest percentage (53.5 percent) indicated that they spent their activity time alone, while 15.8 percent, 17.8 percent and 12.9 percent respectively, chose the aforementioned categories. When asked to respond to the general question of whether they were members of an organized group or not, 52.4 percent said "yes," 34.7 percent said "no" and 3 percent indicated not applicable.

The types of activities chosen by black older people were important to know. Respondents were given the opportunity to prioritize their involvement into three priority categories. Topic areas in the categories were religious, work related, political, recreational, and meals. Respondents did not list meals as part of the first priority group. The results show 21.8 percent choosing religious activities; 2.0 percent work-related activities, 1.0 percent political; 36.6 percent recreational activity, 1 percent other and 37.6 percent not applicable. Under type of group priority number two, 10.9 percent said that meals were the activities in which they became most involved.

Ethnic composition of groups was an important factor to observe. Most indicated they were involved in groups which had individuals of like ethnicity (37.6 percent), and 30.7 percent indicated not applicable, while 31.7 percent indicated an ethnic mix.

The ethnic older persons indicated that they celebrate holidays which have significance for them as ethnic people. Seventy-six and two tenths (76.2) percent responded positively when asked if they observed holidays related to ethnicity and 18.8 percent said no they did not, with 5 percent indicating not applicable. However, after probing further, 66.3 percent indicated they celebrated most ethnic holidays; 5.0 percent said mostly non-ethnic holidays and another 13.9 percent said both ethnic and non-ethnic holidays, with 2.0 percent and 12.9 percent respectively indicating don't know and not applicable.

In conjunction with looking at the activities of older people and the types of involvements they have, respondents were questioned regarding their church membership. When asked if they were members of a church, 79.2 percent indicated they were and 20.8 percent said they were not.

Ethnicity of friends, which was the same as the respondents, was very much expected from the older black population; 72.3 percent said that their friends were the same ethnic-racial background as themselves and 1.0 percent indicated that their friends were not. When responding to the question of friends of mixed ethnicity, 22.8 percent said their friends were of mixed ethnicity, 1 percent indicated other and 3 percent said not applicable.

The context of their social circumstances.

Researchers were interested in knowing how persons felt about life and tried to get an indication of how people cope as they grow older. There was interest in knowing how things seem to be changing for black older people as they grow old. In that respect, 42.6 percent indicated better, 8.9 percent said the same and 48.5 percent felt that things were getting worse. The thing that seemed to be causing the greatest difficulty according to the priority listing given by respondents was health (48.5 percent). Other things causing great difficulty were: transportation (5.9 percent), income (11.9 percent), language (1.0 percent), personal problems (2.0 percent); age (2.0 percent), other (1 percent), and not applicable (27.7 percent).

Older people are often asked what could change their current situation. The first priority ranking of things that would change the older black person's situation is: government (60.4 percent), individuals (1.0 percent), family (1.0 percent), other (27.7 percent), I don't know (2.0 percent), and not applicable (7.9 percent).

Concepts of Aging

The researchers were interested in determining what black older people considered to be old from a non-chronological perspective. The interest was not only in determining what is considered old, but also who is considered old and who determines when the person is old. Respondents were given the opportunity to respond in ways which they felt were appropriate. Their responses were: physical-mental condition (33.7 percent), dependent on others (5.0 percent), state of mind (41.6 percent), chronological age (8.9 percent), appearance (2.0 percent), cannot work (6.9 percent), and other (2 percent).

The interviewers got the impression that most of the interviewees felt that being old was in the mind and is the way people feel about themselves. The more active they were the less they felt they were getting old. Very few black older people used health as one of the indicators of being old. Withdrawal was the variable that many pointed to as being an indication of old age. They felt that when they could not continue to be active and be intimately involved with family, neighborhood, and personal activities, then they were getting old. The majority of the persons interviewed felt that hard work had been a positive factor, rather than a deterrent in their lives. Work seems to have been the thing that they had valued most and they saw it as an indicator of usefulness and importance in the family and in the community. Several respondents were of the impression that they had lived as long as they had because of hard work and good physical conditioning. In addition, some said you are definitely old when you stop and become inactive.

When you stop being involved with others and presenting yourself in a reasonable way, you will feel old and act old. It is the impression of the interviewees that it is your action and the reaction of others to you that most clearly define your age status in the community and in the family. Often, chronological age is not the important factor.

IV. Discussion

The discussion of findings section encompasses a further presentation of findings outlined in the findings section. There will be a more detailed interpretation of the findings with emphasis on the coping patterns, lifestyles, use of services, and some attention to cultural values of black older people.

The elderly in this study are indeed variable. Many of them stated that the only thing that was missing in their lives was their mate, who had passed on. Many of the respondents were involved enough to be able to share their lives in various capacities, such as foster grandparents, campaigning for their favorite politician and numerous other activities.

The items for discussion will be essentially the same as those taken into consideration in the previous section. The primary difference will be that some of the items may be consolidated for comparison and a more in-depth analysis.

Neighborhood

At first glance, one may question how black older residents have survived the many years of struggling to raise families and to maintain a semblance of neighborhood spirit and involvement. The fact that the sample interviewed had been living in the same area for a mean of 28.2 years emerged as significant within the study. It is often speculated that black older residents would move from their neighborhoods if they could. Most of the residents would not move from their neighborhood if they could. The reasons are quite varied. Extended discussion brought out that many would not move because their homes were paid for, their friends were in the general vicinity, they had children and other relatives close by and they knew how to travel without experiencing discomfort.

For a variety of reasons the residents rated their neighborhood as "good" or "fair" with very few indicating their neighborhood as being "poor." Further implications are that other residents refuse to recognize their physical and social environment as being second-class. They have done their best to maintain their community and neighborhood at the highest possible level within their means. The neighborhood then becomes "good" or "fair" from the standpoint that it is not necessarily being compared with other unlike communities. Feedback indicates that very little of the "fair" or "good" rating of the neighborhood has anything to do with the services rendered to the older residents. This was somewhat demonstrated when respondents were asked to indicate what they liked about their neighborhood. The majority said that they liked people because they were good neighbors with the second highest reason being that they were near family. The next highest response was to being convenient to resources. When probing further regarding reasons why persons do not like their neighborhood, it was shown that less than 15 percent said they absolutely did not like their neighborhood with the next highest single reason being that there was a lack of security and a high incidence of crime in the neighborhood.

It is clear that the older black residents continue to depend upon their immediate neighborhood for social and emotional, as well as physical fulfillment. In spite of what may be defined as inter-city deterioration, both socially and physically, older residents continue to depend upon services and general support systems within their immediate neighborhood.

Housing

Housing is considered a serious problem for older people on a national basis. The location of housing is very important in that many older persons have lived for several years in districts which required high taxes after reaching retirement age and many cannot afford to continue the high taxes and maintenance required on their homes. Many black elderly have not lived in the "so-called" high rent districts, and therefore, at a glance are not faced with the same problems; however, when looking more thoroughly, the same or similar problems do exist proportionally. The fact that 41.6 percent of the respondents in this study actually own their homes and another 46.5 percent are renting is significant.

The data clearly shows that there is a problem for older blacks to get housing repaired, even though, in some instances, there were persons who were willing to exchange sources such as minor repairs for transportation. Materials for repair are quite expensive and as a result, the housing very quickly deteriorates and the older person is gradually forced to sell his or her property and move in with relatives or rent. Several residents have not moved frequently and have lived in the same house or apartment for several years. Forty-eight percent have lived in the same house or apartment for eleven or more years, and 21.8 percent have been in the same house or apartment for twenty or more years.

There are several reasons given by the study group for the older black person remaining in the same house. They are in neighborhoods where relatives and other friends reside and have learned to cope with daily problems confronting them. Most have been able to negotiate the informal helping systems in order to help them cope.

Monthly payments for housing are somewhat high when compared to the income of respondents. When payments for rent or house notes are taken under consideration, there is proportionally little left to take care of repairs and other responsibilities that go along with owning a home or renting. The range of monthly payments is very broad. Less than $50 per month was paid by 2.0 percent and 1.0 percent paid from $200 through $249 per month for housing. These findings are very similar to findings in other studies which point out the high proportion of the elderly income that goes for housing alone.

Living Arrangements

Interviewees indicated that many black older people lived alone. Few lived with children or other relatives. Some who had children lived near them, but not with them. Several interviewees were proud of the fact that they could live alone and do not have to be "in the way" of their relatives or children. Many of the older black persons expressed concern about being alone as they get older, but were clearly comfortable with their current living arrangement.

Interactional and Coping Patterns

Family and kin often are the primary source for emotional support in later years. Older people are expected to attach a relatively higher value to the emotional aspects of life as other social functions diminish. They are expected to develop a greater orientation to effective, expressive and affectional goals. Consequently, the family and kinship system becomes the major institution for the social participation of elderly people. At the time of life when emotional security is so greatly challenged, one's family and kin are expected to provide the necessary support for one's morale or well-being (Butler, 1973:57-58), and personal supports in time of stress. One way of thinking suggests that the availability of goods and services through the urban administrative structure serves to enhance isolation and alienation for the more neighborhood-restricted older persons. The underlying assumption is that older people have access to and actually use the services made available and are therefore less dependent upon family and friends.

Support systems of the inner-city or urban elderly blacks increasingly involve a complex of services provided by the family and significant others, and sources offered by large-scale organizations, whether they are governmental or voluntary. It is the government, whether local, state or federal, that provides the basic services for older people in crucial areas such as health, transportation and income maintenance. Regardless, the family continues to meet the more idiosyncratic human needs of the older persons.

Knowing the location of family of the respondents helps to better understand their support systems. The fact that 7.9 percent of the respondents have children in the home and 5.9 percent have grandchildren or great-grandchildren in their homes gave some indication of who represents their basic support system. Children, grandchildren and great-grandchildren living at home does not guarantee older people security, paraphysical support or emotional support. The study does not ascertain why family member continue to live in the same residence with the older persons. Very often, families resided in the same dwelling because of economic situations and it is not primarily in the interest of lending support to the older person.

In order to receive support from relatives, it is not necessary for persons to be residents of the same house. The data brings out the fact that 5.9 percent of the respondents have brothers or sisters living in the immediate neighborhood and 18.8 percent had brothers or sisters living in the county of San Diego. On the other hand, those with children, grandchildren or great-grandchildren living in the neighborhood or in San Diego County were in greater numbers than those with brothers and sisters living in the neighborhood or in the county. The highest percentage was 34.7 for those with children living in San Diego County, with the next highest percentage at 26.7 percent for those with grandchildren or great-grandchildren living in San Diego County. When comparisons are made between those with brothers and sisters living outside the county, it becomes very clear that the most immediate support was from brothers and sisters living outside the county. When further comparisons are made, it is evident that the potential for more support comes from children, grandchildren and great-grandchildren who may live nearby in the county.

There are instances in which support comes from relatives or friends who are outside of the city or possibly the state and that the support comes in many forms. Monetary support can be provided by individuals living anywhere in the country while intimate emotional support can normally be provided by those who are nearest. Again, being near does not mean living in the same block or the same residence. Nearness must be measured by the time it takes to go from one point to another.

Employment

Indications are that respondents were happy to be employed if they were in good health. Feedback from interviewers indicates that there was a diversity of occupations in which the black elderly respondents have engaged in the past. Education and training levels dictated the type of employment blacks have had the opportunity to participate in. The traditional domestic and general labor type of work seems to be very much a part of the employment picture for elderly blacks in this study. The employment pattern has also been in part created by a high degree of racism in the economic and educational segments of the society.

Many of the female respondents had been employed as domestic workers. Since most of the respondents are females, there is a tendency to develop a skewed picture of the type of employment in which older blacks have been involved and are capable of. It is not the older black female alone who has worked as a domestic. Many older black males have also been employed as domestics and their responsibilities included working as servants, gardeners and other related jobs. Traditionally, survival meant accepting manual employment.

The data in this section indicates that the older black person has continued to have an active work life. It is significant in that 94.1 percent of the respondents had worked in the past. Again, since 57.4 percent of the respondents were female, the indication is that females had to work to support their families; and of those respondents who were not currently working, 8.9 percent said that they had a spouse who was working. Many of those who are currently working are doing so because they are not apparently at the retirement age. Implications are that those who are now in their early and mid-fifties may not have the extreme need to work upon retirement, as many of those persons in the sample who are currently much older. Pensions and other security plans will provide a minimal income for some of the persons in the lower age group.

Speculations are that the longer an older person or spouse has not been working, the more services they actually need. The data showed that 60.4 percent of the sample has not been working from 5-10 years. During that span of time they had come to expect a new level of service involvement; if they are involved in the formal service system.

Feedback from the interviewees is that they do not expect their children or grandchildren to fill the same important patterns as themselves as a result of being able to vie for employment which will provide better insurance and pensions. Therefore, they will guarantee security during their retirement years.

Health

Many older black persons have no history of regular attendance at the physician's office. Indications are that many tend to go more now they have gotten older. Some of this can be attributed to the fact that there are more services available for older persons in their neighborhood. Greater emphasis is also placed on providing information and education to the elderly, and a large percentage of the population receives some type of assistance, whether it be MediCal, Medicare or Social Security. Another factor to take into consideration is the additional transportation service in neighborhoods affecting most of the population under consideration. Most do not have an extensive support system through relatives, immediate family and friends to provide the paramedical assistance they may have received in their younger years. Services provided by churches played an important role in educating older members about health services and health care. Many ministers have expanded traditional services to include messages such as "Doctors can heal by working through the Lord" or "You can be healed by prayer and doctors."

Of those responding, 53.5 percent felt their health status was "fair," which is an indication that the study population was not overly concerned about health. More than 17 percent said that they were probably in "poor" health. Another interpretation of this data is that many older blacks may not have had their consciousness raised to the point where they are examining their health status closely enough. Many may be of the opinion that there is nothing they can do to better their health status; therefore, pay little attention to it.

Beyond determining the respondents' conception of their health status, the researchers wanted to find out to whom they turned when they needed help.

The overwhelming majority (63.4 percent) said that they still turn to a family member for help. The number of persons turning to family seems to be somewhat high. The population is not a rural or social suburban population; therefore, it will seem that individuals would have reasonable access to transportation systems and to medical facilities; on the other hand, this also tells us that medical facilities and access to transportation for reaching medical facilities may not be as accessible as we have envisioned. The 7.9 percent who indicated that they used a professional agency or person in time of sickness was exceptionally low; the interpretation of this data may be that the individuals have not given much consideration to whether they are in good or bad health. At the same time, the fact remains that there is a large segment of black elderly not using professional services or getting professional advice.

Respondents had the opportunity to indicate why they did not seek the assistance of professional medical personnel. Feedback is that the greatest fear is of illness being diagnosed and the consequences of those illnesses. Again, this raises the question of degree to which any of the black older persons have had exposure to adequate and correct information regarding, particularly, illness and the durability of certain illnesses.

It was clear that many of those being interviewed needed to be in a hospital, but had not been for many reasons. (Need of hospitalization is an observation made by interviewers.) Several people expressed fear of doctors and other professional medical personnel, because they have not had ongoing contact with the medical system(s). Some openly admitted that they did not go because they did not know what the doctors or nurses might do. There was fear of not wanting to become experimental subjects for hospitals. There is a great deal of suspicion that blacks are continuing to be experimented on to improve the health of others in our society. The feeling was that too much of this type of activity has been permitted in medical institutions for too long.

Income

In 1969, the medium income for elderly blacks was substantially below that for elderly whites. For example, an elderly white family could expect to have $4,884 per year, while blacks could expect to have $3,322 per year. Elderly blacks who lived alone had less income, and nearly a third lived on less than $1,000 a year. White elderly living alone were not exceptionally well off, but generally had nearly twice as much money as blacks in the same age group. The census also brings up the fact that the median income for the total black population for males 65 and over in 1969 was $1,725 and for females, $1,079. Goldstein (1971) said that elderly blacks are likely to arrive at old age with a few accumulated assets and lower Social Security benefits, if any at all. The older black male is more likely to seek some security benefits prior to 65 years of age. In most census regions, except the South, the tendency toward early benefit status is not significantly different by race; however, after 65 years of age Anglos are more apt to receive Social Security at a higher rate than blacks.

Most respondents in this study felt that their financial situation was "fair" (57.4 percent). Only 25.7 percent said their financial situation was "poor." When the mean monthly income is examined, $299 represents a higher monthly income than the national average for blacks in 1970. The statistics do not mean that the financial situation for the San Diego sample is exceptional. Consideration must be given to the fact that this sample includes persons who are still working and are under 65 years of age and older. The maximum of $1,000 per month for anyone in the sample gives more reality to the financial picture based on the education level alone. It is reasonable to expect some of the sample to earn up to or above $1,000 per month.

Sources of income were varied with a high percentage (79.2 percent) receiving income from Social Security. The fact that 20.9 percent said they received a monthly average income from $209 to $250 and 26.8 percent said they received from $252 to $300 per month, verifies the implication that most of the black elderly received income which comes from Social Security. The working respondents bring the 35.9 percent receiving $334 or more per month to a relatively high level.

It is difficult to consider income alone without taking into consideration factors such as education, type of employment, pension benefits, and several other related factors. Without examining the data presented it tends to indicate that the older black San Diegans are financially in better shape than the national average. The base income for the nation's black elderly is exceptionally low. It is reasonable to provide either a differential increment in public income benefits or reduce the cost of public services.

The interviewees were quite willing to discuss income and wanted the interviewer to know as much about the economic situation they were in as possible. Most of the people anticipated the interviewer asking about income and few hesitated to share the actual amount of income.

One interviewer observed that people on fixed incomes may be able to live better during the entire month if they knew how to distribute their funds. A large portion of older black persons have never had to budget for an entire month. It is conceivable that budget planning based on an average low income would be meaningful. A service like this would be helpful to many of the black older people.

Activities

There is a direct relationship between the type of activities in which older persons engage and the type of employment and level of income they have had throughout a lifetime. Older blacks have not had to face some of the problems of many other groups because of their relatively lower income and work experiences. Work has been the catalyst for many of the activities in which the majority of our population engage.

Activities can be defined as the range of involvement outside of employment with which black elderly find themselves associated. Leisure can easily be a synonym for activities as used in this study. Generally, activities for elderly blacks have centered around doing things with their families and friends, and most have never developed a traditional concept of recreation. In the white society, emphasis is usually placed on hobbies and activities such as golf, tennis, bridge, horseback riding, sailing, flying. Some of these activities are not easily related to by most black elderly because of the lack of exposure. If some were exposed to these activities, they quite often did not have money to continue with them. Blacks over a period of time enjoyed church activities, family picnics, cards (not bridge), and talking or just getting together to express themselves. The net result is that many can continue to do the majority of the things they have always done because the activities cost very little. Religion is often pointed out as one of the main involvements of black older people. Many black elderly indicate that they are only continuing a trend that has been an ongoing part of their lifestyle. They indicate that church attendance and church activities have been a sustaining factor in their lives and that they spent a lot of time in church and working in church activities. Some said that attending church is a spiritual involvement and others say it is a way of life. Some actually said that they would go to church more if they were not ill or immobile. Church activities, unlike many others, for the black elderly gave them high status and a respectable position in the church, as well as in the community.

There is no doubt that isolation is one of the greatest fears of persons who are in the process of growing older. One of the concerns of many service organizations is how to get the black older person out and involved in organized activities. The approach may not be to the liking or understanding of many black older people. It is quite possible that the approach be one of in-reach, which means black elderly should not only be approached to become involved in activities on site, but time should be spent in familiar surroundings in order to give them a feeling of security as they become educated or aware of the possibilities for involvement. It is quite possible for service agencies in the community to have in-reach persons who will spend time familiarizing the older person with center activities or community-based activities. The responsibility of the in-reach person will be to go with the older person to a particular facility and introduce them to other older persons there and even spend time familiarizing them with the ongoing activities.

The respondents indicated that they spent most of their time (53.5 percent) alone, while 15.8 percent and 17.8 percent spent it with their families or with friends respectively. This finding further supports the contention that an in-reach service would be meaningful for persons like those in this sample. When the percentage of persons spending time with families and friends (33.6 percent) is combined, it is done not equally to the percentage of persons spending time alone. The hypothesis that family and the relatives fill the major gaps in the life of elderly black persons does not hold. Isolation is a major problem for most groups of older people, and this data indicated that it is no different for the black elderly.

When respondents were asked if they were members of any type of organized group, 62.4 percent said they were and were given the opportunity to prioritize the types of groups to which they belonged. In the first priority grouping, 36.6 percent said the groups they were associated with were recreationally related. Speculations are that some of the recreational activity is actually church involvement. Those indicating religion as a type of group activity as the number one priority category was 21.8 percent, which was lower than expected.

Many respondents (37.6 percent) preferred to be associated with those of the same ethnicity. Another 31.7 percent said they did not care if the ethnic composition was mixed. Another 30.7 percent did not have preference. The implication of this finding is that approximately one-third of the elderly blacks to be served in areas similar to the San Diego area could be expected to participate in activities or service settings in which there are ethnically mixed persons.

Concept of Aging

The purpose here is to begin to look at oldness from the perspective of the black older persons. Black persons were asked to describe who and what is considered to be old and further what determines when the person is old. Responses were varied and had very little direct implications for major differences in ethnicity when looked at alone. The unexpected finding was that 41.6 percent said that the state of one's mind determines when one is old. Most related it to senility or the inability to think coherently, as being the true sign of being old. Another 33.7 percent said that physical-mental conditions determined when one was old. These impressions no doubt help to determine how older persons react to their immediate environment. The reality may be that many black persons are not chronologically old according to our traditional definitions but are physically and mentally old because of the lack of adequate health and social services over a period of time.

There may be reverse effects if many black older people do not see themselves as being in poor physical/mental condition or in poor mental health. They may not take advantage of some of the services provided for older people in their neighborhood. Feedback from some of the interviewers is that many black older people do not say that they are old because of the negative connotations that go along with being designated as such. If the majority feel that they are active and responsive to the environment around them, then they are less likely to say that they are old or act old according to stereotypes even if they are 80 years of age. It is also important to note that only 2 percent felt that appearance was highly significant in defining what was old. Normally, appearance is very important and is one of the factors which most people readily attribute to determining when one is old. This finding indicates that the black elderly are looking beyond the physical.

Transportation

Transportation systems are basically oriented to getting people to and from work areas rather than to and from shopping areas, social services, medical facilities or areas where friends and relatives reside. Cost of transportation is one of the primary prohibitive factors. The older population can sometimes find means of transportation either public or private, but cannot afford it. Walking as a means of transportation is also a problem because of the rapid decline in physical skills. As pedestrians, those in urban areas have difficulty negotiating the on-pushing traffic and competing with the traffic signals.

Transportation problems are somewhat the same for those who live in inter-city, suburban and rural areas. Much of the isolation suffered by older people is due to inadequate transportation. It is nonetheless ironic that black older people are forced to low income areas which unfortunately is synonymous with poor transit service. The high fares and reduced service of transit companies makes it nearly impossible for many older people in "out-of-the-way" places to adequately utilize the service.

Respondents in this study prioritized their means of transportation and in the first priority category, the majority (49.5 percent) indicated that the automobile was the primary means of transportation with 41.6 percent indicating public transportation. This finding is quite similar to that of older people in general in that most continued to depend on the private automobile. Only 4.0 percent indicated that walking was their primary means of transportation in the first priority grouping. In order to determine the degree of dependency, respondents were asked to indicate whose automobile was used. A relatively high percentage (39.6 percent) had their own automobile. In order to determine if respondents were driving their own automobiles, they were asked if someone else drives and 39.6 percent said someone else does. From the data, it is not clear whether or not the same 39.6 percent are those who own automobiles. Speculation is that is not true, there is only 1.0 percent who said they borrow an automobile when needed.

Most important is that 88.1 percent said that transportation is usually available. They did not indicate for what reasons transportation was available. The implications were that transportation was available for respondents to take advantage of as needed. Further, 43.6 percent of the respondents said that they turn to a family member for transportation assistance as their first priority and 29.7 percent indicated that they turn to friends as their first priority. One interpretation of the response regarding available transportation is that most black elderly were saying that family members or friends had transportation which could be made available for their purposes.

Black elderly in the inter-city areas, like others, must depend upon the ability to travel for acquiring the essentials of life such as food, clothing, medical care, and in some cases, employment. Adequate travel provides an opportunity for involvement in spiritual, recreational and a variety of cultural activities. The lack of adequate transportation seems to have a direct bearing on the degree to which elderly blacks participate in community activities.

Nutrition

Diet habits of black elderly have often been considered to be unique or different when compared to the older Anglo person. This comparison has been made with elderly blacks rather than with other ethnic people because it is expected that blacks would have diet habits similar to those of the Anglo population. The literature is beginning to review several works (Brewer, et al., 1974) which note that a large percentage of older black persons have diets which resemble the Anglo diet more than the stereotypes indicate. It is also becoming more apparent that older blacks do not adhere to the stereotypes of the so-called "soul food" diet (Stanford, 1973).

The aforementioned literature indicates that many black older people feel that they have very well-balanced diets. The Brewer (1974) study shows that 75 percent or more of the respondents said that they regularly eat fruit, dairy products, a variety of vegetables and meats. About 60 percent of the sample indicated that their diet habits had changed only slightly in the last 30 years.

There is great concern regarding the number of meals older people have per day. The respondents in this study generally have two or three meals per day. Only 6.9 percent indicated that they have one meal per day. The highest percentages (57.4 percent) said that they had two meals per day, while 35.6 percent indicated three meals per day. The reasons for the majority having two meals per day are varied. One of the primary reasons could be that older people sleep later and go to bed earlier than they did while working. The fact that many live alone and eat alone may have an effect also. Of those responding, 40.6 percent indicated that they eat alone and 36.6 percent said that they eat with one other person.

The finding that 63.5 percent of the older blacks in the study typically eat mixed or non-ethnic meals has implications for nutrition facility operators. Those who ate mostly "ethnic foods" were 27.7 percent of the sample and those who said that they mostly ate non-ethnic foods were 7.9 percent.

It is important to note that 27.7 percent of the sample said that they had a special diet and only 1.0 percent said that they did not. The majority (71.3 percent) said a special diet was not a concern to them. The implication here is that the black older persons can easily participate in meal programs without a great regard for preparing special diets or for preparing the so-called "soul food" in great quantities.

According to the findings, 80.2 percent of the respondents had meals prepared by themselves or someone else in the home. Others had arrangements which included a community nutrition setting, an adult friend, neighbor or relatives or another type of special arrangement. It is significant that persons using community central nutrition sites are only 3.0 percent of the total sample. This indicates that meal preparation is one area in which the older black person is dependent upon the extended family and community setting for an important phase of his or her daily existence. To further support the idea of the extended family being an important link in the support system, 55.4 percent of the respondents said that they turn to family members for food as their first priority, while another 24.8 percent said that they turn to a friend as their first priority.

The data indicates that older blacks are coping very well in the area of nutrition and getting their meals prepared; however, there is an evident need for nutrition program directors to begin more extensive methods to include older blacks in nutrition programs. Much of this can be accomplished through appropriate education in activities in the community. The black older people, like others, should be protected from harmful nutrition practices.

Life Satisfaction

Life satisfaction is relative to the types of the experiences older persons have had throughout life. It is very closely related to one's philosophical point of view and cultural values. Life satisfaction for this study was based on the premise that older blacks have experienced particular things that have had either a negative or positive impact on their life. The intent here was to determine the extent to which they felt things have changed for better or worse during their lifetime. The percent indicating that things were better (42.6 percent) was very close to the percentage of those saying that things have gotten worse (48.5 percent). The remaining respondents felt that things had remained the same. Speculation is that those who feel that things are changing for themselves and their people are those who, in fact, take advantage of services and other program offerings in their immediate neighborhood and the community in general. Part of the response in the negative might be that people have had negative experiences with regard to services provided or they may not konw of the availability of certain such services.

Too often, program planners determine what would be effective for older people without directly consulting with them. The older persons in this sample were asked what things could make the most positive change in their current situation. The first priority was government (60.4 percent). The implication is that most of the black older people are of the opinion that the government, at multiple levels, can influence their lifestyles more than anything else. Those indicating that family would be most important were only 1.0 percent. This finding implies that the government has the greatest opportunity to influence some of the service utilization habits of the black elderly. This does not mean that the government should take advantage of the fact that there is a degree of dependency; it should look at this as an opportunity to provide good programming and services to those who want to utilize them.

There are other elements to life satisfaction which have little to do with services or the availability of services. The older black respondents had indicated that they were relatively satisfied because they had learned to cope with their life situations. Again, their faith in God and that, "God will take care of all things" gives them the encouragement and stamina to go on. Many see the ability to cope with life as their major source of satisfaction and do not need much else.

Services

Social scientists, planners, and researchers talk of social services as if there were a common definition. The perceptions and operational expectations of social services are vastly different for a variety of individuals, as well as organizations. When talking with many black older persons about adequacy or inadequacy of social services in their neighborhoods, it becomes eminently clear that they are not certain about what is being asked of them. For the purpose of this discussion, the operational definition provided by Tobin, et al. (1976) will be used.

> Social services generally include those benefits that are granted by or received from extra-familiar institutions, usually outside of the normal procedures of the market place. Social services are not limited to disadvantaged persons or groups, nor are they necessarily related to a breakdown, real or imagined of the family, the church, and other social institutions.

Three operational functions of social services are delineated. They are socialization and development; therapy, help and rehabilitation; and access information, advice and referral. Information discussed in this section of the study has particular importance for helping to bring about more effective social service. In order to assist the elderly black person in determining his or her service needs, they were asked if they could think of the types of help they needed that was not available. The question was posed in this fashion because it was known that many older people did not respond readily when asked about service needs because of the vagueness of the definition of services. Respondents were asked to categorize and prioritize their needs that were not currently being filled. The highest priority in the first category was more social programs at 30.7 percent. The highest priority in the second category was again more special social programs at 5.0 percent. The most significant findings were that 58.4 percent of the respondents in the first priority grouping said that the question was not relevant to them. Speculation is that many did not fully comprehend what was being asked and did not know what could be included under the rubric of social service.

Participants were asked if they knew of things that agency workers providing services should know or be aware of that would help provide better services. A few (20.8 percent) had very strong feelings about some of the things that agency personnel should know and be aware of. They felt that they should be more courteous and patient in their work and should have more knowledge of the needs of their clients. There was the feeling that there was not nearly enough emphasis and attention given to the cultural or ethnic specific needs of the respondents.

Formal agencies played a very important role in the lives of most of the older people. The black elderly (75.2 percent) indicated that agencies do play a part in meeting their social and physical needs. The help received most was medical care. Health and medical care was responded to as being the highest priority (61.4 percent) by the respondents. The second highest area was finance, with 4 percent of the respondents so indicating.

Considerable speculation has been made about the extent to which black older people used formal agencies. Respondents were asked if they were using or have used formal agencies or if they will use formal agencies. Nearly half (49.5 percent) said that they are using or have used formal agencies. Another 37.6 percent said that they would use formal agencies and only 1.0 percent said that they would not use formal agencies. The fact that only 1.0 percent said that they would not use formal agencies and 37.6 percent said that they would, means that there is a vast number of older blacks who would take advantage of social services if they were available or if they were aware of them.

In order to better understand the total helping system in the black elderly community, respondents were asked who would they help and to describe the type of help they would give. First, it was determined whether the person actually helped others when asked the question, "Do you help others?" Sixty-nine and three-tenths (69.3) percent said that they did and 30.7 percent said that they did not. Many of those who did not were physically able to do so or were living in situations where it would be inconvenient. The frequency of helping others was also determined. Respondents were asked whether they helped others more often, sometimes, or very little. Their responses were: 26.7 percent, 21.8 percent, and 30.7 percent respectively. Those indicating that they helped often, sometimes found themselves in the position of being the primary link between the person being helped and the service agency.

Persons who were helped most often were friends or neighbors (54.5 percent), with family members being second at 8.9 percent. It was expected that church members or those associated with the church would have represented more than 5.5 percent. The data indicated that older black persons providing help gave help to those who were physically closest to them. The type of help given by the majority of the respondents was physical/chores (15.8 percent); in time of sickness (16.8 percent); with the second and third highest responses being to transportation and financial help at 10.9 percent and 12.9 percent respectively. The pattern tends to one of mutual support and assistance between the older person, family and friends with minor assistance from public agencies.

The most important inferences to be made from this data are that services must be accessible and usable. The findings indicate that black older people depend upon individuals and serivces nearest to them. Indications are that if older blacks knew more about the types of services, they would be more likely to take advantage of them. In addition, they would act as liaison or linkages between friends, neighbors, and family that need specific types of services.

Interviewers indicated that some of the respondents had very good ideas about the form of assistance they could receive through public institutions. At the same time, they did not know how to proceed to get some of the assistance. There was feeling that some of the services would be used if there were a better understanding of how to tap the resource without losing personal dignity. Most of the older black persons felt that they had made it without the help of someone "uptown" up to this point and saw no reason to become dependent upon them at this time.

One drawback in working with social service organizations and agencies is that the terminology and jargon is often confusing. The older people interviewed could not define in their own minds what the interviewers mean by social services. The terminology is somewhat foreign. Social service is the term given by professionals and others working in certain areas. Most of the black older people did not take time to consider whether what they needed was a social service or not. They readily define the so-called "social service" by what their immediate need is, i.e., eye-glasses, prosthesis, hearing aid, food.

Interviewers were also interested in getting impressions of how persons shared their resources. It was clear to them that there was no community or family pressure to share available resources. In spite of that, however, most interviewees wanted to share what they were able to.

Help comes most from the family or close friends and neighbors. A high percentage of persons mentioned the church as the institution which provided the most help. Even though the church was indicated, it was not mentioned as often as the interviewers would have expected. Traditionally, blacks as well as other ethnic groups have been said "to take care of their own." Blacks in most neighborhoods and communities were taking care of their own because, for many reasons, the social service systems did not reach into the communities and villages where blacks were forced to live. There just were no other support systems to tie into. Helping was not as difficult a year ago as it is now. Helping has become more difficult because of the great movement of young people from many rural communities to suburban and urban areas and also the movement of many older people to inter-city areas. There was a time when older blacks could depend on the quick response of younger people in their neighborhoods for assistance.

Educational Level

Education refers to the level of formal education through an educational institution. Assumptions are made about the level of education of many black older persons and the impact of the education on their ability to use service systems. Assumptions are also made about correlations between education and income levels of black older people. This discussion is not designed to answer questions about income levels and services, but will address some of the implications of education related to awareness and use of services.

The number of persons having formal education was significantly high (89.1 percent). The mean number of years of formal education was 8.9 percent with a maximum number of years being 20. The mean number of years is somewhat consistent with the mean shown in the other material related to the black older person.

Learning to read and write has been taken for granted by most persons in our society. However, it is more essential today than ever before to be able not only to read, but fully to comprehend the written word. Many of the black elderly continue to have problems negotiating social service systems or understanding literature which attempts to explain how systems work. Many do not attempt to use services because they do not want to reveal the fact that they have reading or writing problems.

One solution to the problem may be more in-home education for the homebound and more out-reach to get older black adults into education programs. This can be one of the best solutions to making them aware of services and helping them acquire skills to take advantage of some of the social services. Many ethnic older people are given opportunities to take English as a second language. Attention should be given to providing assistance to help elderly blacks understand and fully utilize English as a first language. This would be a giant step toward building self-confidence and encouraging older blacks to go out and challenge the existing social service systems.

Social Involvement

Interviewers found that persons who stay to themselves are usually homeowners and have what they consider adequate income. This same group of persons generally seemed not to use existing services even if they knew about them. This was particularly true of those persons who were healthy and felt they could be independent. The significant point seems to be that this group used public services in time of extreme need. The reason for not going regularly was not necessarily because of the lack of knowledge or because of the fear of going. Transportation was adequate and personal care needs were not a question.

Ethnic Indicators

Persons interviewing made special efforts to refrain from using any particular ethnic identifier when speaking with the interviewees. In most instances, older black persons being interviewed used the concept of "black" as the primary identifier. The fact that many were not comfortable with "black" as the identifier also came through. Others were much more comfortable with the terminology of "Negro." Few continued to use "colored" as the identifier and explained "we grew up at a time when black or Negro was not acceptable and it is hard to change at this point in time." It was pointed out that most older persons who had children or younger relatives around do not resist using "black" as an identifier as much as those who do not. The term has been systematically reinforced by youth. It is significant to note that many black older people use "we" instead of any particular term.

V. Summary Conclusions and Recommendations

Summary and Conclusions

Implications for service delivery to the black elderly are many. The data discussed in this section help to support the notion that there is a need for a service system which can be easily negotiated by all older people. Some of the implications around helping and who helps, point out rather clearly that the majority black older persons look from within their household or immediate community for assistance. The primary helping system as described by the sample for this study continues to be the immediate family, whether seen as nuclear or extended.

Discussions continue around the issue of whether ethnic older people should have services designed to meet their unique needs. Few people deny that there is a need for specific services for some of the ethnic older people in our communities. Some of the literature (Jackson, 1971), indicated that many black elderly may prefer to have their own service systems. If that assumption were further tested according to the findings of the sample, that would seem to be true. The data show that black elderly depend primarily on those services in their immediate neighborhoods and that they tend to engage in activities with mostly persons of their own ethnic-racial background. The debate is not so much whether services should be developed separately, but whether services should be developed in areas that people do not naturally use because of their dependence on things in their immediate environment.

Generally, the findings indicate that the services available and the services actually used by the elderly blacks in the sample are two divergent issues. Services are often available and may even be accessible. The reality is that too many of the elderly in the sample were not aware of the specifics of the services and had they been aware, may have in fact, used some of the services. As was indicated in the body of the discussion section, a major task for service agencies at this point may be to provide out-reach or in-reach to continue to make the black older people aware of what is available and provide means for those who are eligible and willing to take advantage of service opportunities.

General Recommendations

The research project has had many interesting and important dimensions. Recommendations included in this section represent an attempt to outline considerations for a variety of individuals, organizations and disciplines. This effort has meant more than doing a piece of research in the traditional sense. The lessons learned from a methodological and community organizational point of view have been rather pronounced.

The original intent of the study was to look at service delivery systems and their appropriateness for the ethnic older persons in the San Diego metropolitan area. It was soon determined that the service needs and service delivery systems were not necessarily the key to providing better services. Lifestyles, coping patterns, ethnic identity, and cultural values are factors which have a great impact on the actual seeking and utilization of service systems.

It has been the lack of understanding and foresight on the part of public, as well as private, planners and program implementors that this type of research and methodological development has been needed. The data presented in the previous sections and the discussion of those data will provide support for the forthcoming recommendations. The recommendations can be of use to planners, policy makers, administrators, researchers, agencies funding ethnic/minority programs and ethnic and older ethnic people becoming involved in research-survey projects. The aforementioned lists of potential users is by no means exhaustive.

The recommendations outlined below are general in nature and are applicable to a variety of individuals and interest groups:

1. Service providers must be flexible and responsive to individuals and group client needs in order to minimize language and cultural barriers.
2. Out-reach information must be more explicit and presented from the perspective of the black elderly.
3. Research and service must be more interrelated if meaningful and substantive data are to be obtained. It is essential for researchers to be more aware of services and be able to provide directions to potential clients when the need arises. It is important to develop a relationship between the information providers and information seekers for the purposes of research if high-quality and substantive information is to be obtained and eventually validated.
4. Federal agencies should develop more effective means of record keeping and data gathering in relation to ethnic older people to ensure that future funding for programs is adequate. The undercount in the census of ethnics and particularly the older populations has tended to leave responsible program agencies with the impression that there is a limited need for services to the minority ethnic populations. It is essential to have adequate and appropriate demographic data in order to provide an awareness for the entitlements.
5. Federal funding sources should seriously consider the feasibility of developing standards for the design and conduct of training programs for community-based minorities who are interested in being involved in research and research implementation and utilization. Currently there is very little training for paraprofessionals in ethnic communities who represent a wealth of untapped manpower and expertise for the purposes of research. The potential is unlimited in that they would provide an entry into the community with an understanding of the norms and cultural concerns, as well as technical know-how.
6. Sub-populations within the ethnic populations must continually be given special attention in relation to both expanded service and existing service provisions. Services very often exist in the larger community, but sub-populations continue to be unaware of these services or find them inaccessible and often unacceptable. Public services, such as transportation, foodstamp facilities and medical programs are often available in the community at large; however, either because of ineffective communication or language barriers, the services are under-utilized by the black elderly.
7. Provisions should be made for technical assistance to be provided to community-based ethnic groups to assist in the design and development

of research methodology. Research for and by minorities has more often been weak methodologically than ideologically.

8. There should be particular emphasis on training ethnic researchers who will be able to work as professionals in minority communities and provide expertise to translate findings about target populations to responsible planners and programmers. They can also provide consistency in research style, utilization of language and develop formal conclusions directly related to the data.

9. Further research should be conducted on the effect of ethnic identification to the utilization of services for the purposes intended.

10. Research should be conducted to determine the extent to which culturalization and socialization have an impact on the awareness and utilization of public or private services. Further work should be done to validate the instruments used in seeking information regarding ethnic older persons.

11. Systematic and ongoing efforts should be made to involve professional researchers, agency leaders, and consumers in research efforts.

12. Agencies should continue to be encouraged to develop systems of accountability which can reflect the inclusion of minority input.

13. All research projects and programs in aging, to the extent possible, should include components to provide more information and data on ethnic older persons.

14. Serious efforts should be made to ensure that there are minority students in research training programs sponsored by federal agencies.

15. In-service training programs paid for by federal funds should include means of collecting and using data regarding ethnic older people.

As indicated earlier, the recommendations suggested above are not intended to be exclusive. They are only to serve as guides for further thinking and action.

GLOSSARY

Patterns of describing older black persons and their activities and status in our society have been very non-specific. The tendency has been to describe them in terms of the white majority. Some of the terms or phrases described in this section represent an attempt to clarify and perhaps amplify some of the concepts and idea constructs contributed to older black persons.

Old Black. An individual who is chronologically not old enough to be classified in the category of the formal or sanctioned retirement group, but is one who is physically not capable of resonding to social or emotional stimuli as one of his chronologically is expected to. Also, one who holds on to the majority of the ideas about what a black person should do and be from a traditional perspective.

Old, Old Blacks. Persons who are chronologically far beyond the expected age of formal nonwork status and are persons who have not taken advantage of new technology and harbor traditional ideas about social interaction and involvement.

New Old Blacks. Persons who may be chronologically beyond formal retirement status, but have been able to adjust to new technologies, integrated new philosophies, are emotionally involved with change and may or may not be physically involved.

False Acculturation. The illusion of being integrated into a societal framework which rejects the full participation of society members; limited involvement in many essential areas which serve to integrate one into society; utilizing general norms but adjusting and adapting norms to subcultural use and modified participation in prescribed activities.

Service Patterns. The utilization of personal, public and community resources to fulfill in day-to-day needs.

Value Islands. Values and norms that continue to exist within an ethnic group, but have normatively disappeared according to the society as a whole.

Independence. The ability to make social, economical and emotional decisions without the imposition of the enforcement of public laws and regulations which may or may not be meaningful in the ethnic of the older person concerned.

Extended Emotional Support. Knowing that friends, relatives and any significant others, whether far or near in distance, will do all they can to help provide a positive psychological environment. This includes reassurance, encouragement, paying attention to special personal celebrations and being knowledgeable of the older persons' strengths and weaknesses.

Informal/Natural Systems. Unplanned pattern of relationships and interrelationships in a specific environment where services to people in need are spontaneously provided. Such systems are generally based on kinship, employment acquaintanceship, friendship, likeness in philosophy of life or religion.

Informal Providers of Service. Those who give services to person(s) without payment and in response to a specific or general need.

METHODOLOGICAL REFERENCES

Alvarez, Rudolfo. The unique psychohistorical experience of the Mexican American people. *Social Science Quarterly*, 1971, *52* (1), 12-29.

Blauner, Robert, & Wellman, David. Toward the decolonization of social research. In Joyce A. Laher (Ed.) *The death of white sociology.* New York: Vintage Books, 1973.

Campbell, Donald T., & Stanley, Julian. *Experimental and quasi experimental designs for research.* Chicago: Rand McNally College Publishing Co., 1963.

Clark, Margaret, & Anderson, Barbara Gallatin. *Culture and aging: An anthropological study of the older American.* Springfield, Ill.: Charles C. Thomas, 1967.

Cooley, Charles H. Primary groups. In Paul H. Hare, Edgar F. Borgutta, & Robert F. Bales (Eds.) *Small groups: Studies in social interaction.* New York: Alfred A. Knopf, 1955.

Counting the forgotten: The 1970 census count of persons of Spanish-speaking background in the United States. Washington, D.C.: U.S. Government Printing Office, 1974.

Federal Register. Title 45: public welfare, Part 46: protection of human subjects, 1975, *40* (50), 11854-11858.

Garcia, Ernest. Chicano Spanish dialects and education. *Aztlan,* 1971, *2* (1), 67-73.

Glaser, Barney G., & Straus, Anselom L. *The discovery of grounded theory.* Chicago: Aldine Publishing Co., 1967.

Gouldner, Alvin (Ed.). Explorations in applied social science. In Alvin W. Gouldner, & S.M. Miller (Eds.) *Applied sociology opportunities and problems.* New York: The Free Press, 1965.

Hamilton, Charles. Black social scientists: Contributions and problems. In Joyce Ladner (Ed.) *The death of white sociology.* New York: Vintage Books, 1973.

Lofland, John. *Analyzing social settings.* Belmont, Pennsylvania: Wadsworth Publishing Co., Inc., 1974.

Moore, Joan W. Situational factors affecting minority aging. *Gerontologist,* 1971, *2* (2), 88-93.

_____. Social constraints on sociological knowledge: Academics and research concerning minorities. *Social Problems,* 1973, *21* (1), 65-77.

Murase, Kenji. Ethnic minority content in the social work curriculum: Social welfare policy and social research. In *Perspectives on ethnic minority content in social work education.* Boulder, Colo.: Western Interstate Commission for Higher Education, 1972.

Romano, Octavio. The historical and intellectual presence of Mexican Americans. *El Grito,* 1969, *2* (2), 13-26.

Sieber, Sam D. The integration of field work and survey methods. *American Journal of Sociology,* 1973, *48,* 1335-1359.

Solomon, Barbara. Growing old in the ethnosystem. In E. Percil Stanford (Ed.) *Minority aging: Proceedings of the Institute on Minority Aging.* San Diego: The Campanile Press, San Diego State University, 1974.

Stebbins, Robert A.   The unstructured research interview as interpersonal relationship. *Sociology and Social Research*, 1972, *56*, 164-179.

Takagi, Paul.   The myth of "assimilation in American life." *Amerasia Journal*, 1973, *2*, 149-158.

Truzzi, Marcello (Ed.).   *Verstehen, subjective understanding in the social sciences.* Reading, Mass.: Addison, Wesley Publishing Co., 1974.

Vaca, Nick C.   The Mexican American in the social sciences, 1912-1970, part I. *El Grito*, 1970, *1* (1), 53-78.

_____ The Mexican American in the social sciences, 1912-1970, part II. *El Grito*, 1970, *3* (3), 3-24.

Valle, Ramón.   *Amistad-compadrazgo as an indigenous webwork, compared with the urban mental health network.* Unpublished doctoral dissertation, University of Southern California, 1974.

Webb, Eugene; Campbell Donald; Schwartz, Richard; & Schrest, Lee.   *Unobstrusive measures: Non-reactive research in the social sciences.* Chicago: Rand-McNally Co., 1971.

LITERATURE AND THE BLACK ELDERLY

Until recently, little effort has been rendered to incorporate the unique situations of the black elderly into written form. Conversely, contemporary gerontological literature on blacks is either sparse or inaccessible. Therefore, the review of literature is more or less confined to those recent concentrated efforts of a selected few.

Dr. Jacquelyne Johnson Jackson has published many articles pertaining to black elderly. Primary reference is given to a research conference on black elderly (1971). From this conference came one overriding theme: that there exists a need for sound knowledge as a basis for comprehensive planning and action to promote the development and delivery of good services to elderly black folk (Jackson, 1972).

In an article published in *The Gerontologist,* Dr. Jackson discusses the black elderly, provides a brief survey of social gerontological literature concerned with elderly black folk and urges more research efforts to be put forth in the area of black aging (Jackson, 1971).

Daniel I. Rubenstein examines the social participation found among a national sample of black and white elderly, and concludes that there are demographic differences between black and white elderly which impedes the former and enhances the latter their degree of social participation in given situations (Rubenstein, 1972).

Recently, a report written by the County of San Diego, Office of Senior Citizens Affairs sought to illustrate the vast network of existing and future proposed senior citizens services provided by San Diego and its neighboring communities (Office of Senior Citizens Affairs, 1973).

At the other end of the spectrum, George Henderson views the black elderly from an OAA perspective and expounds on the inherent obstacles in the welfare system which sometimes prevent it from effectively serving its black recipients (Henderson, 1965).

Available data pertaining to certain stereotypes commonly held about black folk tended to be invalid when compared with available data on black elderly. The majority of the respondents had less than sixth-grade education and their occupation for the majority of their lives had been either farming or laboring (Jackson, 1970).

Andrew Billingsley traces the extended family as an African cultural carryover and exposes its characteristics which still prevail within black families in this time and space (Billingsley, 1968).

According to Hannah Weihl, the aged of oriental origin differ from those of western origin. A greater number of those of oriental origin reside with their children, more have frequent contact with the children not living with them and the leisure-time activities pattern is much more home-centered and family-oriented. Although the black and Jewish cultures differ significantly, their family structures appear to be very similar (Weihl, 1970).

An African proverb indicative of the feelings of older black people was illuminated in the writings of Jacob Drachler:

> There is no wealth where there are no children. There is true happiness only where there are children. But children are not only a source of happiness. They

are also a great help to their parents. When parents become too old to provide for themselves, they pass into the care of their children and are provided for by them. Thus, children are a source of wealth to the parents and a valuable investment (Drachler, 1963).

Health is a significant factor in determining the longevity of elderly black folk. One stereotype of older black folk is that they are in poorer health than their white counterparts. To the contrary, Dr. Jackson has shown that black elderly "tend to depart from such statistical stereotypes" (Jackson, 1970:144).

Because of the covert and overt racism still in existence within the United States, educational and preferable occupational opportunities were not afforded to the now elderly blacks in their earlier years. Consequently, very few are able to rely upon pensions, savings, annuities, stocks and bonds and the like. They are therefore relegated to dependency upon Social Security and/or public welfare for their existence. In this time of inflation, increasing standards of living levels are not very conducive to the well-being of elderly black folk nor for anyone else.

A paper presented to the National Agricultural Outlook Conference presents some percentages and dollar amounts relative to income, poverty and consumption by and for older people (Brotman, 1972).

When practitioners are engaged in diagnostic evaluation of elderly black folk, a concentrated effort to become and remain aware of the implications of race as well as racism must be maintained for proper treatment. Butler and Lewis concern themselves with the nature and problems, as well as evaluation, treatment and prevention (Butler, Lewis, 1973).

Portions of the proceedings from the Institute on Minority Aging deal with the distinctive background of the behavior patterns of minority elderly persons. An understanding of these patterns is necessary if practitioners are truly to help the "now" generation, as well as future generations to deal effectively with those patterns in order to make old age acceptable as well as comfortable (Stanford, 1974).

Getting to know the black elderly person from literature is most difficult. In the field most related to the social process of aging—social gerontology—very little can be found. Seeking the black elderly in writing on family life is equally nonproductive. Not only are the elderly missing, but Billingsley (1970) also finds "no area of American life more glaringly ignored, more distorted, or more systematically disvalued than the black family life."

The position and status of the elderly in African societies had great importance for the whole social system. In part because they were between man and God, grandparents obtained position and status because they stood only a little lower on the ladder of infinity. Children obtained from the grandparents of both sexes family history, folklore, proverbs and other traditional knowledge. Grandparents were perceived as the living links with the past. This meant that the family provided for the maintenance of the elderly, which, coupled with self-worth, provided an aspect of longevity which enabled the elderly to be elderly.

The American system of slavery systematically destroyed this by denying families the relationships they held prior to becoming Negroes. This was done by omitting the elderly from the infamous "middle passage" (transportation from the African coast to the Caribbean and North American coasts), dissolving established families, and creating new ones with members who were unable to communicate with one another because of language unfamiliarity.

Although the traditional family was destroyed, somehow some of the cultural traits survived, but with new emphasis on the grandmother more than the grandfather. She became, once again, the library of the accumulated folklore and spiritual beliefs and was always on hand when black, as well as white children were born. All orphaned and abandoned children were taken under her care for their well-being and upbringing.

Theoretically, emancipation meant that the harsh life to which black folk were subjected would become less harsh because they were supposedly able to participate in the mainstream of American life. This interpretation was contingent on the fact that blacks were now able to compete with white folk for jobs and political positions which had earlier been denied them.

> Some planters held back their former slaves on their plantations by brute force. Armed bands of White men patrolled the country roads to drive back the Blacks wandering about. Dead bodies of murdered Negroes were found on or near the highways and byways. Gruesome reports came from the hospitals— reports of colored men and women whose ears had been cut off, whose skulls had been broken by blows, whose bodies had been slashed by knives or lacerated with scourges. A veritable reign of terror prevailed in many parts of the south. (DuBois, 1969)

Grandmother stressed the importance of being independent and self-reliant. She was well aware that there would be very many helping hands for her offspring and their offspring once they left her sphere of protection and ventured into the hostile, larger and very often violent society. She stressed cooperation between her family as a means by which her family would be able to survive, grow and develop.

> There was no "generation gap" between the Black grandmother and her descendents after the era of slavery had ended. She had learned so much from experience—how to deal with the dominant society and survive, how to remember what had happened and relate that to other happenings (oral history). She was also an authority on the mysteries of life—having babies and caring for them, curing common illnesses, preparing tasty, although not always healthful, meals from meager foods. If there was not enough food for the family she often pretended not to be hungry so that other family members could eat her share. Younger people listened to her and valued her advice. As she grew older, she was even more respected and esteemed for her knowledge and for her contributions to people, for she willingly helped neighbors as well as her own kin. In fact, it was not uncommon for the Black grandmother to accept and rear, in addition to her own grandchildren, a niece, a nephew, a cousin, or even an orphan who had nowhere to turn for societal aid. (Crisis, 1973)

As black families began the migratory process from the rural areas to the urban areas in the South, North, East and West, the grandmother often assumed the role of parent of her grandchildren while her children and their mates could make a start in the urban environment. She knew, as had her predecessors in the post-emancipation society, that it would be difficult for her children to meet the obligations of child-rearing while searching for work and housing. She therefore raised the grandchildren to make things somewhat easier for her children. When her children were well-established, she would return the grandchildren to them. She continued to help by having her grandchildren stay with her during the summer. The results were that a sense of family, knowledge of roots and a feeling of belonging with someone were maintained even though geographical location separated the family.

When the time came (usually during the young adult years), today's elderly black folk migrated to the urban centers, seeking economic advantages and social outlets. Instead they were greated with dilapidated housing, poor wages, a higher cost of living, poor diet and health resources.

Although the earliest and most trying times are behind today's elderly black folk, they are still affected by those forces. It is difficult, if not impossible, to try to remain in or to re-enter the labor market (*Social Casework*, 1965:212).

The black older persons' retirement plight has been tragic and humiliating. The Social Security retirement benefits are directly proportioned to one's life earnings, and the black elderly's benefits tend to be virtually nonexistant. Many had to apply for Old Age Security to sustain their existence, and regarded it as the only source of retirement income.

Shelter, which consumes the greatest portion of the limited income, takes precedence over all other priorities. As a result, very little is left for food, which causes an insufficient diet, which, in turn, causes poor health and a decrease in homogenity.

In spite of the many adverse conditions which have unequivocally influenced elderly black folks' lives, they appear to have remained a distinct and functional segment in American society.

Selected References for Literature and the Black Elderly

Billingsley, A.   Black families and white social science. *Journal of Social Issues,* 1970, 26 (3), 127.

——————   *Black families in white America.* Englewood Cliffs, N.J.: Prentice-Hall, Inc., 1968.

Brewer, P., De Voe, L., et al.   *The older black San Diegan.* Unpublished master's essay, School of Social Work, San Diego State University, 1974.

Brotman, H.   *The fastest growing minority: The aging.* Paper presented at the National Agricultural Outlook Conference, February 24, 1972.

Butler, R.N., & Lewis, M.I.   Black versus white. *Aging and mental health.* St. Louis, Missouri: C.V. Mosby Company, 1973.

Drachler, J.   *African's heritage.* New York: Macmillan Company, 1963.

DuBois, W.E.B.   *Black reconstruction in America: 1860-1880.* New York: Atheneum Publishing Company, 1969.

Goldstein, S.   Negro-white differentials in consumer problems of the aged, 1960-61. *Gerontologist,* 1971, *11,* 242-249.

Jackson, H.   National goals and priorities in the social welfare of the aging. *Gerontologist,* 1972, *11,* 226-231.

Jackson, J.J.   *Proceedings of research conference on minority group aged in the South, October 1971.* Durham, North Carolina: Center for the Study of Aging and Human Development, Duke University Medical Center, 1972.

_____.   Negro aged: Toward needed research in social gerontology. *Gerontologist,* 1971, *11,* 52-57.

_____.   Aged Negroes: Their cultural departures from statistical stereotypes and rural-urban differences. *Gerontologist,* 1970, *10* (2), 140-145.

Kahn, A.J.   *Social policy and social services.* New York: Random House, 1973.

Litwak, E.   Extended kin relations in an industrial democratic society. In E. Shauas & G. Streib (Eds.) *Social structure and the family.* New Jersey: Prentice-Hall, 1965.

Rubenstein, D.I.   Social participation of aged blacks: A national sample. In J.J. Jackson (Ed.) *Proceedings of research conference on minority group aged in the South, October 1971.* Durham, North Carolina: Center for the Study of Aging and Human Development, Duke University Medical Center, 1972.

Social Casework, April 1965, p. 212.

Solomon, B.   Growing old in the ethno-system. *Minority Aging,* 1974, *2,* 9-15.

Stanford, E.P.   *Suburban blacks: A case study overview.* Paper presented at the 1973 Gerontological Conference, Miami, Florida.

_____.   *Minority aging: Proceedings of the Institute on Minority Aging.* Center on Aging, San Diego State University: The Campanile Press, 1974.

The Crisis Magazine, January 1973, pp. 19-21.

Tobin, H.S.; Davidson, S.M.; & Sock, A.   Models for effective service delivery. *Social services for older Americans.* The School of Social Service Administration, The University of Chicago, 1970.

Weihl, H.   Jewish aged of different cultural origin in Israel. *Gerontologist,* 1969, *10* (2), 146-150.

Weiss, G.   *Southeast San Diego health study.* County of San Diego, 1969.

ANNOTATED BIBLIOGRAPHY ON BLACK AGING

Books

Bourg, C.J.   A social profile of black aged in a southern metropolitan area. In J.J. Jackson (Ed.) *Proceedings of research conference on minority group aged in the South, October 1971.* Durham, North Carolina: Center for the Study of Human Development and Aging, Duke University Medical Center, 1972.

The speaker reported on an empirical study of older blacks in Nashville, Tennessee. The study noted how the social environment differentially affects aged blacks. In addition, he notes that we do not have sufficient information about the nature and function of extended households containing black aged, nor have we yet adequately conceptualized arrangements existing within black households.

Carter, J.H.   Psychiatry, racism, and aging. In J.J. Jackson (Ed.) *Proceedings of research conference on minority group aged in the South, October 1971.* Durham, North Carolina: Center for the Study of Human Development and Aging, Duke University Medical Center, 1972.

The talk portrayed the general lack of interest psychiatrists have had in aged blacks, the need to train both black and white psychiatrists to more effectively treat mental health problems confronting some of the black aged, and the devastating effects of racism on emotional health.

Eisdorfer, C.   Research, training, service and action concerns about aging and aged persons: An overview. In J.J. Jackson (Ed.) *Proceedings of research conference on minority group aged in the South, October 1971.* Durham, North Carolina: Center for the Study of Human Development and Aging, Duke University Medical Center, 1972.

The address concentrated on research, action, training, and services relative to minority group aging. Most important was the emphasis on building better techniques, of "searching" in lieu of "researching," and of proceeding from a strong base of knowledge and task awareness instead of merely plunging into the dark.

Hill, R.   A profile of black aged. In J.J. Jackson (Ed.) *Proceedings of research conference on minority group aged in the South, October 1971.* Durham, North Carolina: Center for the Study of Human Development and Aging, Duke University Medical Center, 1972.

The discussion provides a statistical profile on the black aged, It was stated that aged black suicide rates are considerably lower than those of aged whites. This example probably best exemplifies the historic fortitude and resilience of black people in America. It emphasizes the need to focus research attention on the aged black now living, for we shall probably not see "their likes" again.

Hirsch, C.   A review of findings on social and economic conditions of low-income black and white aged of Philadelphia. In J.J. Jackson (Ed.) *Proceedings of research conference on minority group aged in the South, October 1971.* Durham, North Carolina: Center for the Study of Human Development and Aging, Duke University Medical Center, 1972.

The study indicated household and kinship similarities between low-income black and white aged. It noted the significant proportion of contemporary childless aged blacks and presented many other racial comparisons of social characteristics as well as projections for the future.

Jackson, H. C.   The white conference on aging and black aging. In J.J. Jackson (Ed.) *Proceedings of research conference on minority group aged in the South, October 1971.* Durham, North Carolina: Center for the Study of Human Development and Aging, Duke University Medical Center, 1972.

The keynote address focused principally on relationships between the National Caucus on the Black Aged and the 1971 White House Conference on Aging, as well as provided information about the goals for the former and the need for the latter to become specifically concerned about needs or problems common to all aged and those unique to particular racial and ethnic minorities.

Jackson, J.J.   Research, training, service, and action concerns about black aging and aged persons: An overview. In J.J. Jackson (Ed.) *Proceedings of research conference on minority group aged in the South, October, 1971.* Durham, North Carolina: Center for the Study of Human Development and Aging, Duke University Medical Center, 1972.

The article focused primarily on three policy concerns emanating from the author's empirical research on the aged black in the South. (1) Existing programs often fail to recognize both the inability of the black kinship network to meet the needs of older blacks and the fact that matriarchy is not a dominant family pattern among blacks; (2) measures should be taken to assure that the most needy blacks are selected for public housing; (3) there is a need to reduce the minimum age requirement for black males as primary beneficiaries of OASDHI so as to reduce unfair racial gaps as they currently exist.

McDowell, A.   Health data on aging persons. In J.J. Jackson (Ed.) *Proceedings of research conference on minority group aged in the South, October 1971.* Durham, North Carolina: Center for the Study of Human Development and Aging, Duke University Medical Center, 1972.

The discussion concentrated on manpower needs in health and statistical data, structural and functional aspects of the National Center for Health Statistics and upon various morbidity and mortality rates by age, sex, and race in the United States. A prime reason for our lack of data about aged blacks may well be because there is a shortage of investigators trained in health and statistics. There is a need to urge federal generation of relevant data.

Ramsey, E., Jr.   Nutritional research, training, and services relative to aging and aged blacks. In J.J. Jackson (Ed.) *Proceedings of research conference on minority group aged in the South, October 1971.* Durham, North Carolina: Center for the Study of Human Development and Aging, Duke University Medical Center, 1972.

The article focused on the need for more attention in the area of nutrition for older blacks. It pointed out our dearth of data in this area, and the need for more data about daily activities and energy expenditures of aged blacks, as well as alerting us to perhaps a frequent lack of sufficient iron and calcium in the diet of many aged blacks in the South.

Rubenstein, D.I.   Social participation of aged blacks: A national sample. In J.J. Jackson (Ed.) *Proceedings of research conference on minority group aged in the South, October 1971.* Durham, North Carolina: Center for the Study of Human Development and Aging, Duke University Medical Center, 1972.

The lecturer explored patterns of social participation among a national sample of black and white aged. The white aged were more likely than black aged to reside alone or to reside solely with spouse and less likely to experience intergenerational household continuity. He called for more baseline demographic data for program planning and development and encouraged substantially more research on blacks.

Stern, R.S., Phillips, J.E., & Rabushka, A. *The urban elderly poor: Racial bureaucratic conflict.* Lexington: Health and Co., 1974.

The results of the survey of this study indicated that to be old and black is substantially different from being old and white. Blacks are poorer, live in less satisfactory accommodations, are poorly educated, etc. Blacks report social wants at a rate of two to eight times as great as whites.

Articles and Journals

Clemente, F., & Sauer, W.J. Race and morale of the urban aged. *Gerontologist,* 1974, *14* (4), 342-344.

Analyzed racial differences in morale for comparable samples of 721 black and 211 white residents of Philadelphia aged 65 and over, using Philadelphia Geriatric Center Morale Scale. Race did not emerge as even a moderate predicator of morale. The outcome was explained by M. Messer's (1968) argument that elderly blacks view old age as a reward in itself, and J.D. McCarthy and W.L. Yancey's 1971 contention that presumed racial differences in morale have received little actual empirical support.

Domeny, P., & Drinrich, P. A reconsideration of Negro-white mortality differentials in the United States. *Demography,* 1967, *4,* 820-837.

The article summarizes the results of an investigation of the validity of Negro-white mortality differentials as reflected in a series of official United States statistical tables published at the turn of the century. It suggests that official figures grossly underestimate the early childhoo- mortality among blacks. The data indicates a higher life expectancy at birth than was really the case. A very technical article, it may be useful as a historical document.

Ehrlich, I.F. The aged black in America: The forgotten person. *Journal of Negro Education,* 1975, *44* (1), 12-23.

Reviews research on needs and psychosocial characteristics of black aged 65 or over and emphasized the need for training gerontologists, especially blacks, to provide educational activities for aged blacks and to study their subculture. It is concluded that educational institutions and the federal government should be instructed to educate aged blacks and to develop black gerontologists.

—————— Toward a social profile of the aged black population in the United States. *International Journal of Aging and Human Development,* 1973, *4,* 271-276.

A stratified random sample of black men and women aged 70 and over was developed in two high-rise, age-segregated urban housing units. Normative activity was classified in terms of three life styles: alone, reciprocal, and non-reciprocal. Involvement with others tended to increase with age. Findings of this study suggest the desirability for encouraging flexible lifestyle options.

Himes, J., & Hamlet, M. The assessment and adjustment of aged Negro women in Southern cities. *Phylon,* 1962, *25,* 139-148.

The study showed that although 100 of the aged black women varied markedly in level of adjustment, they were concentrated at the upper end of the adjustment scale. Differences of level of adjustment were related to variations of employment experiences, home ownership, education, and health conditions. The evidence from this and other studies suggests that these variables comprise clusters of factors that are significant in the experiences of aged persons — one of the few articles devoted to older black women.

Henderson, G.   Negro recipients of OAA: Results of discrimination. *Social Casework*, 1965, *46*, 208-214.

The article explores factors that are unique to aging blacks. The data is based on an exploratory study of 100 aged blacks who were recipients of Old Age Assistance grants in Detroit, Michigan. The author predicts that with continuing increases in the black average life expectancy, and continued racial discrimination, there will be an increasing number of aging blacks living on public assistance. The article gives a brief history of racial discrimination in the United States. Generalizations are based on only one study.

Jackson, J.J.   Aged blacks: A potpourri towards the reduction of racial inequities. *Phylon*, 1971, *32*, 260-280.

This paper focuses specifically upon: (1) the grandparental roles in the contemporary urban Southern setting and certain implications of those roles relative to social and cultural conditions of aged blacks; (2) a discussion on the National Caucus on the Black Aged; and (3) development of an argument to reduce the minimum age requirements for Old Age Assistance disability, survivors and health insurance so as to reflect the disparities in life expectancy rates. It provides a framework for innovative change to help meet the needs of the black aged.

_____. Aged Negroes: Their cultural departures from statistical stereotypes and rural urban differences. *Gerontologist*, 1970, *10* (2), 140-145.

The article contends that the black aged tend to depart from statistical stereotypes that suggest their marital statuses are significantly different from those of white aged; that their life expectancies are typically less than whites (they may be longer at the later age periods); that they differ from whites by the importance put on their families, etc. Some variables that may be useful in distinguishing between rural and urban black aged are: income sources, material possessions, health, family, friendship ties, church participation, and attitudes toward death and aging.

_____. The blacklands of gerontology. *Aging and Human Development*, 1971, *2*, 156-176.

The selection is a review of the literature on the black aged. The focus is developmental psychology and race, and social patterns, policies, and resources. It provides excellent bibliographic reference. Suggested introductory reading in minority aging.

_____. Help me somebody! I's an old black standing in the need of institutionalizing! *Psychiatric Opinion*, 1973, *10* (6), 6-16.

States that racism adversely affects the delivery of effective health care resources to a majority of aged blacks. This population does not have sufficient access to the institutions most appropriate to their conditions or to adequate psychiatric and other mental health resources. Blacks had a greater probability of long-term confinement in mental hospitals than the majority population. Remedial measures are suggested.

_____. Marital patterns among aging blacks. *The Family Coordinator*, 1972, *21*, 27.

The article describes spouse dominance patterns among a sample of older urban married blacks in Durham, North Carolina. The study showed that matriarchy was not the dominant patterns among black husbands and wives. Marriage is not a dominant pattern among black women over 65. Two-thirds of black women over 65 are widowed. The article provides insight into older black marital adjustment.

_____. Negro aged: Toward needed research in social gerontology. *Gerontologist*, 1971, *11* (1,2), 52-57.

This article provides a brief survey of the literature in social gerontology related to aging blacks. It also critically evaluates the research that has been done on the black aged. In addition, it discusses some of the most important research problems and areas of concern in black aging with reference to the need for future research.

_____. Sex and social variation in Negro older parent-adult child relationships. *Aging and Human Development,* 1971, *2,* 96-107.

Lacken, C. Aged, black, and poor: Three case studies. *Aging and Human Development,* 1971, *2,* 202-207.

The study is based on case studies of three older blacks using in-depth interviews in their homes. The respondents were drawn from urban, lower class, age-segregated, highrise apartment complexes located in a Southern urban area. The findings do not attempt to prove or disprove theories about aged blacks but merely stands as a report of each individual's response during an open-ended discussion of their lives.

Lambling, M.L.B. Leisure time pursuits among retired blacks by social status. *Gerontologist,* 1972.

The article discusses the factors that determine the number of leisure-time activities among elderly blacks. It also lists some of the favorite leisure-time activites.

Messer, M. Race differences in selected dimensions of the elderly. *Gerontologist,* 1968, *8* (4), 245-249.

The article studies the difference between white and Negro elderly on the attitudinal dimensions of life satisfaction (morale), feelings of societal integration, and self-conception of age status.

Morgan, R.F. The adult growth examination: Preliminary comparison of physical aging in adults by sex and race. *Perceptual and Motor Skills,* 1968, *27,* 595-599.

The data from this study is derived from the Adult Growth Examination which was based on norms of hearing, blood and dental measures from a sample of several thousand examined in a national health survey of a representative sample of Americans. By dividing the male norms of the national health survey into black and white sub-samples, it can be seen that races are equal in body at age 21, but equality disappears thereafter. Black males 30 years old and over have older body age than their white counterparts. The biggest jump in body age is between 21 and 30, after which blacks hold a 5-year body-age differential until 60.

Rubenstein, D.I. An examination of social participation found among a national sample of black and white elderly. *Aging and Human Development,* 1971, *2,* 172-188.

The article examines older blacks' participation (in comparison with white aged) with family and kin. The analysis is accomplished through the use of demographic data on elderly blacks and whites. The conclusions indicated that the black elderly are no more alone and isolated than the general population of older people. In addition, their emotional state of well-being is no different from that of the white elderly. The article argues that research should be critical in exposing myths and generalities about the black aged.

Shader, R.I., & Tracy, M. On being black, old, and emotionally troubled: How little is known. *Psychiatric Opinion,* 1973, *10* (6), 26-32.

The article exames the frequency of service delivered to elderly blacks by a state- and federally-supported psychiatric hospital and community mental health center. It was found that over a 2½-year period, two-thirds of the patients over the age of 65 were admitted to either in-patient or day-hospital care; only 8 of these were black. Possible explanations for this low proportion of blacks include a frightening perception of mental illness among elderly blacks, a definition of mental illness different from that of whites, and different life expectancy.

Swanson, W.C., & Harter, C.L.   How do elderly blacks cope in New Orleans. *Aging and Human Development,* 1971, *2,* 210-216.

The author developed the following insights based on case studies of elderly blacks in New Orleans: (1) despite the fact that they were generally old, poverty stricken, and in failing health, they did not feel life is unbearable; (2) most could not recall having been confronted with a crucially important problem that seemed to defy solution; (3) they were optimistic which, in part, could be attributed to their religiosity.

Wylie, F.M.   Attitudes toward aging and the aged among black Americans: Some historical perspectives. *Aging and Human Development,* 1971, *2,* 66-70.

The study suggests that black Americans are more inclined than whites to include the elderly in the family structure and to regard the elderly with respect, if not veneration. Blacks seem to be more accepting of their own aging. The origin of the phenomenon is traced through cultural development in Africa and the effects of slavery on black aging.

Documents

The aging and aged black.   Reports of the Special Concerns Sessions, 1971 White House Conference on Aging, Washington, D.C., U.S. Government Printing Office.

The report illustrates the urgent needs of the black aged. It points out the following areas where federal assistance should be directed: education, employment, retirement, physical and mental health, nursing homes, housing, income, nutrition, retirement roles and activities, spiritual well-being, transportation, research, etc.

Other References

Cantor, M.; Rosenthal, K.; & Wilker, L.   Social and family relations of black aged women in New York City. *Program Twenty-Eighth Annual Meeting of the Gerontological Society Louisville, Kentucky, October 26-30, 1975.* New York: New York City Office for the Aging.

A sample of 1,552 black women over 60 was drawn in the inner-city of New York. The study examines kinship structure integration in neighborhood social network and viability of family. The dominant extended family, usually headed by older black women, although a response to constraints of poverty and racism, appears adaptive to the needs of the family members, provides a role for older women and is more positively related to respondents' morale than other family structures.

Yelder, J.E.   *General relationships in black families: Some perceptions of grandparent role.* University of Southern California, Department of Social Welfare, June 1975.

This study investigates themes and variations in the role of grandparents in black families. The role of the grandparent is explored in three dimensions: style of grandparenting, degree of comfort in performing the role, and significance and meaning of the role to the grandparent. The study suggests that although grandparents may not be part of a three-generation household, close family ties exist and are valued by grandparents. Further study is needed of families not living in the same household to enlarge our perspective regarding the kinship network.

Books

Davis, D.   Growing old black. In *Employment prospects of aged blacks, Chicanos, and Indians.* Washington, D.C.: National Council on Aging, 1961.

Jackson, J.J., & Davis, A., Jr.   Characteristic patterns of aged rural Negroes in Macon County. In D.C. Johnson (Ed.) *A survey of selected socio-economic characteristics of Macon County, Alabama, 1965.* Tuskegee, Alabama: Macon County Community Action Office, 1966.

Kent, D.P., & Hirsch, C.   Social and economic conditions of Negro and white aged residents in urban neighborhoods of low socio-economic status. *Needs and uses of services among Negro and white aged,* vol. I. University Park, Pennsylvania: The Pennsylvania State University, 1971.

Riley, M.W., & Foner, A.   *Aging and society,* vol. I. New York: Russell Sage Foundation, 1968.

Sheppard, H.L.   Age and migration factors in the socio-economic conditions in urban and black women. In *New perspectives on older workers.* Kalamazoo, Michigan: The W.E. Upjohn Institute, 1971.

Articles and Journals

Beattie, W.M., Jr.   The aging Negro: Some implications for social welfare services. *Phylon,* 1960, *21,* 131.

Brunswick, A.F.   What generation Gap? A comparison of some generational differences among blacks and whites. *Social Problems,* 1969-1970, *17,* 358-370.

Cairo, C.   Why the National Caucus on the Black Aged? *Harvest Years,* 1971, *11,* 13-18.

Geagin, J.R.   A note on the friendship ties of black urbanities. *Social Forces,* 1970, *49,* 303-308.

──────────.   The kinship ties of Negro urbanities. *Social Science Quarterly,* 1968, *69,* 660-665.

Jackson, J.J.   Kinship relations among Negro Americans. *Journal of Social and Behavioral Sciences,* 1968, *13,* 42-47.

──────────.   Negro aged and social gerontology: A critical evaluation. *Journal of Social and Behavioral Sciences, 1968.*

Jackson, J.J., & Ball, M.   A comparison of rural and urban Georgia Negroes. *Journal of the Association of Social Science Teachers,* 1966, *12,* 30-37.

Jenkins, M.M.   Age and migration factors in the socio-economic condition of urban blacks and urban white women. *Industrial Gerontology,* 1972, *9,* 13-17.

Kastenbaum, R.   A special issue—black aging. *Aging and Human Development,* 1971, *2* (2), 155-231.

Metropolitan Life Insurance Company.   Trends in mortality of non-whites. Statistical Bulletin, 1970, *51,* 5-8.

Orshansky, M.   The aged Negro and his income. *Social Security Bulletin,* 1964, *27.*

Rice, C.   Old and black. *Harvest Years*, 1968, *8*, 38-47.

Smith, T.L.   The changing number and distribution of the aged Negro population of the United States. *Phylon*, 1967, *18*, 339.

Talley, T., & Kaplan, J.   The Negro aged. *Newsletter*, Gerontological Society, December 1956, No. 3.

Documents

U.S. Senate, Special Committee on Aging.   *The multiple hazards of age and race: The situation of aged blacks in the United States.* Washington, D.C.: United States Government Printing Office, 1971.

Lindsay, I.B.   *The multiple hazards of age and race: The situation of aged blacks in the United States.* Washington, D.C.: U.S. Government Printing Office, 1971, Report No. 92.

Lopata, H.Z.   *Social and family relations of black and white widows in urban communities.* Washington D.C.: Administration on Aging Publication No. 25, U.S. Department of Health, Education, and Welfare.

Unpublished

Antenor, J.A.   *An exploratory study of the relation of the adjustment of one hundred aged Negro men in Durham, North Carolina, with their education, health, and work status.* Unpublished master's thesis, University of North Carolina, 1961.

Ball, M.E.   *Comparison of characteristics of aged Negroes in two countries.* Unpublished master's thesis, Howard University, 1966.

Bohanon, T.   *Some considerations of St. Louis Negro aged.* Unpublished master's thesis, circa 1958.

Crocker, M.S.   *An analysis of the living arrangements and housing conditions of Old Age Assistance recipients in Mississippi.* Unpublished doctoral dissertation, Florida State University, 1968.

Davis, A., Jr.   *Selected characteristic patterns of a Southern aged Negro population.* Unpublished master's thesis, Howard University, 1966.

Davis, G.   *The effects of the Social Security Act on the status of the Negro.* Unpublished doctoral dissertation, University of Iowa, 1939.

Dhaliwal, D.D.   *A sociological description and analysis of a non-random sample of low income Washington, D.C. aged Negroes.* Unpublished master's thesis, Howard University, 1966.

Geagin, J.R.   *The social ties of Negroes in an urban environment.* Unpublished doctoral dissertation, Harvard University, 1966.

Gillespie, Michael.   *The effects of residential segregation on the social integration of the aged.* Unpublished paper, University of Missouri, August 3, 1967.

Hamlett, M.L.   *An exploratory study of the socio-economic and psychological problems of adjustment of IDO aged and retired Negro women in Durham, North Carolina.* Unpublished master's thesis, North Carolina College at Durham, 1959.

Hirsch, G.; Kent, D.P.; & Silverman, S.L. *Homogeneity among low-income Negro and white aged.* Paper presented at the Twenty-First Annual Meeting of Gerontological Society, November 1, 1968, Denver, Colorado. (Mimeo)

Jackson, J.J. *Changing kinship roles and patterns among older persons in a black community.* Paper presented at The American Psychological Association, Washington, D.C., September 1, 1969.

_____. *Leisure-time and mental outlook: A comparison of Southern rural aged samples.* Unpublished Ed.D. dissertation, Pennsylvania State University, 1955.

_____. *Retired Negroes: Some empirical findings and impressionistic judgments.* Paper presented at the Conference on Ethnic Differences in Patterns of Retirement, sponsored by the Adult Development and Aging Branch, NICHD, Tucson, Arizona, 1969.

Kent, D.P., & Hirsch, C. *Differentials in need and problem solving techniques among low-income Negro and white elderly.* Paper presented at the Eighth International Congress of Gerontology, Washington, D.C., August 25, 1969.

Nash, G.; Lawton, M.P.; & Sinon, B. *Blacks and whites in public housing for the elderly.* Paper presented at the Annual Meeting of the Gerontological Society, Denver, Colorado, 1968.

Pettigrew, T.F. *The Negro aged: A minority within a minority.* Unpublished paper, Institute for State Executives in Aging, Brandeis University, 1967.

Sherman, E.G., Jr. *Social adjustment of aged Negroes of Carbondale, Illinois.* Unpublished master's thesis, Southern Illinois University, 1955.

Smith, S.H. *The older Negro American.* Unpublished master's thesis, 1966.

Stojanovic, E.J. *Morale and its correlates among aged black and white rural women in Mississippi.* Unpublished doctoral dissertation, Mississippi State University, State College, 1970.

Stretch, J.J. *The development and testing of a theoretical formulation that aged Negroes with differences in community security are different in coping reactions.* Tulane University, New Orleans, Louisiana, 1967.

Thune, J.M. *Group portrait in black and white.* Senior Citizens, Inc., Nashville, Tennessee, 1969.